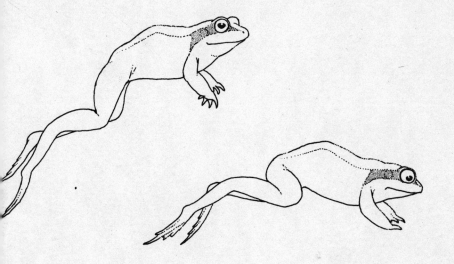

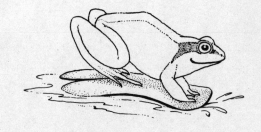

FROGS & TOADS

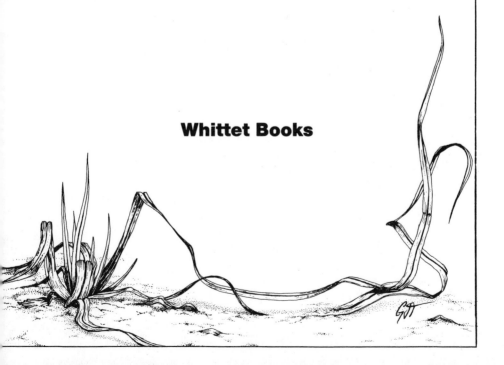

FROGS & TOADS
•TREVOR BEEBEE•

with illustrations by
GUY TROUGHTON

Whittet Books

First published 1985
Reprinted 1989, 1993
Text © 1985 by Trevor Beebee
Illustrations © 1985 by Guy Troughton
Whittet Books Ltd, 18 Anley Road, London W14 0BY

Design by Richard Kelly

British Library Cataloguing in Publication Data

Beebee, Trevor J.C.
  Frogs and toads.
  1. Frogs   2. Toads
  I. Title
  597.8   QL668.E2

  ISBN 0–905483–38–3

Typeset by Inforum Ltd, Portsmouth
Printed in Great Britain by WBC

Contents

Preface

Just about everybody knows what a frog is and what it looks like. It is also common knowledge that frogs grow up from tadpoles, and that tadpoles hatch from clumps of 'spawn' looking remarkably like tapioca puddings. This much about frog biology seems to have become an established ingredient of our childhood education; for most of us, though, that is about it. How many people, for example, would claim to be able to tell the difference between a frog and a toad? Yet the more we learn about these much maligned animals, the more fascinating they become. Their lives are more complicated than almost any other creature you can think of, certainly more so than any other vertebrate (the back-boned or 'higher' animals: fish, amphibians, reptiles, birds and mammals, including ourselves). Starting life in water and then changing over to spend most of it on land involves enormous alterations in body shape and function, so much indeed that it is natural to wonder how frogs and toads have been able to survive at all in competition with other more advanced animals. Yet we can see their success every spring, with tadpoles in ponds, lakes and ditches all over the world.

Frogs and toads remain enormously successful, and one of the challenges to people studying them is to understand why this is so. Students of frogs and toads are called 'herpetologists', the name arising from a Greek word 'herpeton', meaning a creeping or crawling thing – not all that appropriate for frogs which can jump many times their own length. Some people think that herpetologists are almost as peculiar as the creatures they study, an image not always easy to dispel. Herpetology covers an interest in all amphibians and reptiles: not just frogs and toads but also newts, salamanders, lizards, snakes, crocodiles and tortoises as well as a few more obscure creatures like the tuatara of New Zealand. To clear up one unfortunate recent confusion, herpetology has nothing whatever to do with herpes – a family of viruses which inflict rather unpleasant and antisocial symptoms that have become notorious lately.

This book is an attempt to widen interest in frogs and toads, and perhaps recruit a few more herpetologists along the way. Mainly it is about British and European species, but there is such variety in behaviour and ecology among the many types found all over the world that I have mentioned some of the more eccentric species from distant parts when they serve as interesting illustrations. There is still a lot to learn even about the common varieties of frogs and toads, and finding out new things about them can be surprisingly easy. Furthermore, some species have declined in numbers so much recently that their conservation has become an important issue, requiring the help and support of as many people as possible. Dispelling prejudices against these fascinating (and very useful) creatures is one of the objectives of this book; to do this may help to ensure that frogs and toads will be around for the education and delight of future generations of children (and adults) just as they have been in the past. Another aim is to present the important (and some not so important) facts about frogs and toads in a digestible form: lots of short bits, more or less complete in themselves, will, I hope, make for easy and casual reading. As the reader, you will be the judge of how successful these aims have been. I can only hope that you will find frogs and toads to be as interesting as I have done in my extended childhood searching out and studying them.

University of Sussex, 1984   *Trevor Beebee*

Acknowledgments

It would be difficult to list everyone who has, at some time or other, stimulated my interest in amphibians, and I must apologize in advance to anyone who thinks he should be on this page, but isn't. Fellow members of the British Herpetological Society have been instrumental, and include Brian Banks, Stephen Bolwell, John Buckley, Keith Corbett, Richard Griffiths, John Griffin, Tom Langton, Mike Preston and Jonathan Webster. It has been a pleasure to talk toads with Arnold Cooke, Tony Warburton and Jimmy Rose and various members of the Amphibian Ecology Group such as Paul Gittins, Rob Oldham, Tim Halliday and their colleagues. The British Herpetological Society, Nature Conservancy Council, Natural Environment Research Council, Carnegie (UK) Trust and World Wildlife Fund have been kind enough to support research and conservation projects, for which I am duly grateful. My thanks go to Pat Morris, whose idea it was that I might write this book, and to my wife Maggie without whose interest the more eccentric aspects of herpetology (tadpoles in the bath) would have been embarrassing if not impossible.

The name game

'Frog' and 'toad' are very old words. Nobody knows exactly how old, but their origins certainly go back at least to Anglo-Saxon times. Thus the old English 'frogga' and 'forsc' were clearly related to the old German 'frosc' and the old Norse word 'froskr'. Likewise 'toad' relates to the old English 'tadige' or 'tadde', though beyond that its origins are unknown. When many people today have difficulty telling them apart it may seem a bit surprising that frogs and toads were distinguished from one another so long ago; our illustrious ancestors were obviously better observers of nature than we might have given them credit for. That other distinctly amphibian word, 'tadpole', first appears in 15th–16th-century English as 'tadderpolle' – an easily recognizable hybrid of 'toad' and 'polle', the latter meaning 'head' and referring of course to the all-head-and-tail appearance of tadpoles.

Naturally there have been many local words for frogs and toads too, though most have long since fallen into disuse. 'Paddock', invoked for frog or toad indiscriminately, was one of the most widespread, especially in northern England, and even features in a 17th-century rhyme by Herrick, 'A child's grace':

> Here a little child I stand
> Heaving up my either hand
> Cold as paddocks though they be
> Here I lift them up to thee
> For a benison to fall
> On our meat and on us all.

The natterjack toad may derive its name from its remarkably loud croak, or perhaps from the Anglo-Saxon word 'naedre' meaning 'lower', which was applied willy-nilly to all crawling creatures (thus 'a naedre' or 'a nadder' became 'an adder'). The natterjack has enjoyed a number of parochial names, such as 'yellowback' or 'running toad' in parts of East Anglia, 'Birkdale nightingale' in the Southport area of Merseyside and 'Thursley thrush' in Surrey. Even so, I sometimes wonder about the actual use of these colourful titles; in Ireland, natterjacks are supposed to be known to the locals as 'black frogs' but during a recent visit there our enquiries about 'black frogs' were met with blank astonishment. Of course herpetologists get used to that kind of reaction, but it was obvious that this particular folk name was far from widely known and we were treated much the same as people who talk about pink elephants after closing time.

The scientific names of the three British species are more recent, and have been generally agreed only within the last hundred years or so. Frogs, genus *Rana*, and toads, genus *Bufo*, are direct interpretations of the Latin names for the two groups ('genus' means group name). Even the Romans could distinguish frogs and toads, quite probably for dietary reasons (see p. 110). Eating a toad instead of a frog could have rather nasty consequences (see 'poisons', p. 58). The common frog is *Rana temporaria*, meaning the 'temporary' or 'summer' frog because it's not seen in winter when it is hibernating. Mind you, this name could be applied to just about all amphibians in temperate countries and seems curiously inappropriate for the species which is more active in cold weather, and breeds earlier, than any other European amphibian. The common toad is simply *Bufo bufo*, and the natterjack *Bufo calamita*. *Calamita* is from the Latin *calamus*, a rush or reed, and refers to the male natterjack's habit of hiding among reeds when croaking during the breeding season. Considering the many more remarkable features possessed by natterjack toads this appears to be another example of unimaginative naming, but for the purposes of science it doesn't matter a lot what title is given. The essential point is that people like me, with scant knowledge of languages other than English, can recognize articles about a species by seeing the Latin name in the title or text of some foreign magazine or journal. It's an aid to international communication.

So what *are* the differences between frogs and toads? Well, you could say that frogs are greenish-yellow, slimy and jump a lot, and that toads are plump, warty and tend to waddle along. As far as the British species go this would be quite a good basic guide, except that the natterjack often runs like a mouse. Internally, toads of the genus *Bufo* have a bone and cartilage arrangement in their shoulder 'girdles' which is different from that found in frogs of the *Rana* type. So if we were just to look at the British species it would be quite easy to come up with clear-cut distinguishing features. Alas, the whole pattern breaks down if we start to look beyond the English Channel, and it has to be said that the popular notions of 'frog' and 'toad' are really fraudulent without a universal basis in classification. We need look no further than the so-called European tree frog, *Hyla arborea*, to find an example of how the simple view can fail dismally. Here is a green, smooth-skinned hopper (leaper even) which, when you look inside, turns out to be much more closely related to toads (*Bufo*) than to frogs (*Rana*). And there are lots more exceptions. However, it's only really necessary for scientists to fret about the vagaries of classification; such details need not be of concern to most folk. Suffice it to say that there *are* logical ways of classifying 'tailless amphibians' (which is what frogs and toads are), collectively referred to as 'anurans', which give a good idea of who is related to whom without bothering about names like 'frog' and 'toad' at all. In Britain, all we need to be able to do in practice is to tell apart our meagre three species, and this is really a very simple matter (see p. 21). It's the bird watchers, with their hundreds of species and varieties, who need to worry about the finer points of classification; British herpetologists have no problem here.

The pop-eyed frog

Even experts sometimes get into trouble with names. A few years ago one herpetologist wrote a tongue-in-cheek article describing the 'pop-eyed frog', a peculiar flat species found on roads when cars had just passed by. Unfortunately he took the joke too far by giving these traffic victims a scientific name, Rana magnaocularis. *It was rapidly pointed out by correspondents to the next edition of the journal that this joke scientific pseudonym had already been given to a real frog in Mexico several years earlier. All very embarrassing to author and editors alike, because things of this kind can cause serious confusion to later generations of readers — or even current ones not well versed in the English language.*

How many kinds are there?

By any standards, frogs and toads are pretty successful animals. Like us they are vertebrates, complex creatures with segmented backbones; and although vertebrates form only a small fraction of the kinds of life on Earth, they are quite clearly among the most sophisticated. This isn't just human chauvinism, there's no doubt that any visitor from outer space would quickly reach the same conclusion. At the last count there were altogether more than 4,000 species of amphibians in the world, a very similar total to that estimated for mammals. Amphibians are a very distinct group of vertebrates: their characteristic features are a naked skin (no fur, feathers or scales), a lack of proper ribs, and a unique method of reproduction. Amphibian eggs do not have hard shells or membranes to stop them drying up, so they either have to be laid in water (the usual situation) or kept moist in some other way (such as in the mother's body) while they develop. In evolutionary terms, amphibians sit neatly between the (more or less) completely aquatic fishes, and the (more or less) completely land-living reptiles. Fish are the most varied group of vertebrates, with more than 23,000 species, but all these figures pale into insignificance when compared with some of the non-vertebrates. Among the insects, for example, beetles alone run into hundreds of thousands of types.

All but a few hundred of the 4,000 or so amphibians are anurans, i.e. frogs and toads. The remainder are mainly newts and salamanders, along with a few burrowing, wormlike creatures called caecilians. Amphibians can be found on all the continents of the world and all the major islands, though they never reached some of the remoter ones such as Pacific atolls. No amphibians live in the sea or can survive long in seawater, and no doubt this explains their absence from these very isolated places. Like just about all other creatures, amphibians are most abundant in the warmest places in the world, especially tropical rainforests. There must be lots of species still to discover in the remoter parts of South and Central America, and some of those we already know about can be pretty bizarre by European standards. One South American type, *Pipa*, lives in dirty, muddy brooks and looks as if it has been run over by a steamroller. Eggs of this species are pushed into holes in the female's back, and her skin literally grows over them to protect the developing tadpoles. These later eat their way out, apparently not causing their mother any distress by doing so – in fact it's doubtful whether she even notices. On the other hand quite a lot of tropical frogs take much more care over their offspring than our British ones do; their behaviour amounts to a quite different reproductive strategy, in which only a small number of eggs are laid, but these are protected in some way to increase their chances of survival. A common method is to make some sort of foam 'nest' for the tadpoles to grow up in, out of the way of nasty predators

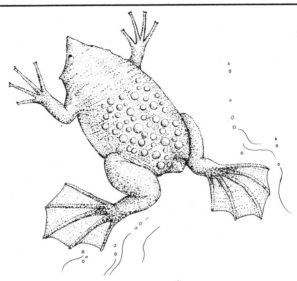

Surinam toad

such as beetle larvae (and other frogs). One species even makes its nest in the branches of a tree, overhanging a pond into which the tadpoles eventually drop to complete their growth. Probably the weirdest way to procreate is demonstrated by a frog in Queensland, Australia, which was only discovered a few years ago. This very rare animal simply swallows its eggs and turns its stomach into a 'growbag', starving itself for the duration of the tadpoles' development and finally regurgitating fully formed froglets. Tadpole growth can be monitored just by X-raying the females periodically.

It isn't just in the field of reproduction that foreign frogs show so much variety. In the Australian deserts there are impressive adaptations to drought, some frogs having huge water bladders that can keep them alive for years beneath the sand until the rains come again. The African clawed toads, *Xenopus*, must be among the most abundant vertebrates in the world, being found, in one form or other, throughout the continent except for the Sahara. These animals are highly aquatic, and lay enormous numbers of eggs – 10,000 or more – each season. One reason for this is that the tadpoles are able to eat microscopic algae in the ponds, a food source the adult frogs cannot tap directly. So the frogs produce lots of taddies to harvest the algae, and then set about eating their own tadpoles to reap the benefits. Back in South America, a daytime walk through a rainforest will often reveal large numbers of tiny, brightly coloured frogs going about their business apparently indifferent to the attentions of other animals, which can't fail to notice them. Their bright blues, reds and yellows are in fact warning colours, just like those on a wasp or bee; these frogs produce in their skin a number of devastatingly effective poisons, and would-be predators have learnt to leave them alone. Unfortunately for the frogs the natives caught on to this a long time ago, and make use of the skin secretions to tip their arrows when hunting game – hence their common name, 'arrow poison frogs'.

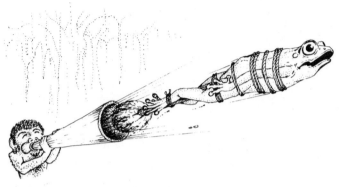

Amphibians alive today don't come very big. The giant salamander, *Megalobatrachus*, of China and Japan is the largest, reaching 5 feet (160 cm) or so long. This beast is still caught for food in its native lands, and specimens are occasionally donated to the London Zoo; it has a similar recent history to the giant panda, being given away by the Chinese to zoos around the world, but rarely breeding under captive conditions. The goliath frog, *Conrana goliath*, of the West African Cameroons is the largest anuran, with a body length of about 1 foot (30 cm). This is a rather rare animal, seldom seen in captivity.

Closer to home, even Europe has its oddities. Perhaps the most interesting is the midwife toad, *Alytes*: as the name suggests, father helps deliver the eggs and carries them entwined around his back legs until hatching time. It also comes as a surprise to learn that a new species of toad, previously known only as a fossil, was discovered in Europe as recently as 1980. *Baleaphryne* turned up in, of all places, the tourist stronghold of Majorca. Europe, being a relatively cold place, has only 45 species of amphibians, compared with 150 mammals (remember that numbers are about equal in the world as a whole). In the inhospitable extremities, like Britain, the discrepancy is even more marked, with 40 or so mammals and a mere 6 native amphibians. Of these, 3 are newts and the others frogs (1) and toads (2) as we have seen in the previous section.

So Britain is a pretty unpopular place in amphibian circles, and you might imagine it to be a frustrating country for a herpetologist to live in (the situation with reptiles is just as bad). It's certainly true that herpetology is more of a mainstream activity in Europe, and even more so in North America (which has more than four times as many amphibian species as the whole of Europe), than it is in the United Kingdom. Fortunately there is still a lot to learn, and a great deal of general interest, even just with our handful of species. Things could be worse. If you live in Ireland, for example, they certainly *are* worse; the Emerald Isle has only three species of amphibian, and a single reptile.

New Guinea monster

Most disciplines of natural history have their folklore, and herpetology is no exception. Some mammal lovers still pay at least half-hearted attention to expeditions after yetis, Siberian mammoths (until recently anyway) and South American giant ground sloths; ornithologists long for a living Moa, and so on. The equivalent for the frog fraternity, some years ago, was a giant animal reputed to live in the forests of New Guinea. At least one paper was written about this hypothetical beast, apparently known to local tribesmen as 'agak' or 'carn-pnay', depending on whom you talked to. An expedition with native bearers and all the usual paraphernalia was mounted to provide specimens of agak, which was expected to be bigger than the existing world champion (Conrana goliath *of the Cameroons, see opposite*). *Needless to say, the outcome was negative and at least for the time being Africa can keep its frog entry in the* Guinness Book of Records.

Evolution of frogs and toads

Amphibians living on Earth today are pale shadows of their former selves. There was a time when the ancestors of our humble frogs and toads could rightly have thought themselves masters of the planet. Admittedly this was an unimaginably long time ago, even before dinosaurs towered over the landscape. Some 300 to 350 million years have gone by since the prototype amphibians first crawled from the water, starting out as rather poorly modified fishes. Until recently it was thought that no relatives of these ancient creatures still survived, but imagine the excitement when, just before the last war, a living specimen of such a fish – the coelacanth – was caught in the sea near South Africa. Since then a number of these 'living fossils' have come to light (local fishermen had always known about them, naturally) and scientists fall over each other to study the latest specimen. Fins on these fishes look more like lobes, showing a crucial stage in the evolution of limbs for crawling out onto land. Although amphibians weren't the first living things to conquer dry land as some textbooks imply (many plants, and invertebrates such as crustaceans beat them comfortably), their appearance on land was certainly an evolutionary milestone from our point of view. These first amphibians were direct ancestors of humans as well as of all modern frogs and toads. The traumatic change from living in water, with gills, to living on land, with lungs, is re-enacted every year when frogs and toads breed, and in midsummer their tadpoles 'metamorphose' into froglets and toadlets. The analogy shouldn't be pushed too far though; the ancestors of frogs looked like fish, not tadpoles.

For over 100 million years the ancestral amphibians were the dominant form of life on land, and many different kinds developed. Some grew very large, but there were no true frogs or toads at this time. Folklore has it that salamanders can walk happily through a blazing fire – quite untrue of course, the poor creatures would

Ichthyostega: *an early amphibian that lived about 350 million years ago.*

frizzle immediately – but there is an irony to the legend. The early amphibians looked rather like modern salamanders, and their peak was during the so-called 'carboniferous' period; they inhabited those same ancient jungles that we now burn, as fossilized coal, in our fireplaces and power stations.

Primitive amphibians did well because they had no serious competition, but all good things come to an end. The evolution of the first reptiles, some 200 million years ago, signalled the start of a long downhill path for the amphibia. It wasn't entirely bad news; amphibians responded to this pressure by continuing to evolve and the first real frog-types put in an appearance around this time. Much later the arrival of birds and mammals added to their difficulties, but it's a sure sign of their resilience that there are still so many frog and toad species alive today. They are far from redundant, with many groups continuing to evolve rapidly – a real vindication of the basic design.

What about our own frogs and toads? Well, frogs of the genus *Rana* seem to be very much on the up in evolutionary terms. They appeared relatively recently (perhaps 30–40 million years ago) and are still undergoing rapid variation and production of new species. 'Rapid', of course, doesn't mean decades, or even centuries; a quick evolutionary change takes a million years or so. A sensible comparison is with other animals like crocodiles; they are at the other extreme, and haven't changed appreciably in more than 100 million years, as we can see from their fossils. Toads of the *Bufo* variety probably date back about 50–60 million years, and are thought to have originated in South America. They are therefore more primitive than *Rana* frogs. As often happens in evolution, *Bufos* went through a period of rapid expansion and variation after they first appeared, and then settled down to be relatively static. Common toads and natterjacks have probably been separate species for at least 15 million years, longer ago than man and apes went their separate ways.

More recently the most important events for frogs and toads (apart, perhaps, from the appearance of man) have been the Ice Ages. All the European species were driven south as the glaciers advanced, and none survived in Britain at the height of the cold. Mostly they hung on in places like Italy and Spain, and then spread north again when the ice retreated 10,000 years ago. Sea levels were lower then and Britain was joined to mainland Europe, so there was nothing to stop frogs literally hopping across what is now the Channel. As the ice melted, the sea rose, and about 9,000 years ago finally cut us off. Britain's years of splendid isolation had begun, and any frogs that hadn't made it by then were doomed to remain foreign.

Cold-blooded killers

Frogs and toads, like reptiles, insects and many other groups of creatures, are often referred to as 'cold-blooded' animals. This is not a very sensible phrase, but it is true that there are important differences between 'cold-blooded' and 'warm-blooded' beasts. 'Warm-blooded' means that body heat is generated internally, using food as the fuel. Only birds and mammals are warm-blooded by this definition, and it's an expensive luxury. Up to 90% of our food intake is needed for heat production alone, but of course it does mean that we can live and be active anywhere from the Equator to the Arctic. Cold-blooded animals should really be called 'variable-blooded', or something similar, because when they are active their blood is not particularly cold. The body temperature of a common toad in summer will be around 27°C, and a natterjack 30°C, compared with our own 37°C. The real difference is that frogs and toads don't get their warmth from burning up food, but rely mainly on background (infra-red) radiation or direct sunshine to heat them up.

This may sound dodgy, and of course it does mean that in winter they get very cold and just have to stay put somewhere until the environment warms up again. But it's much less of a problem for tropical species, and there is the great advantage that one needs much less food to keep alive. That is why you can have so many frogs or toads living in quite a small area, where the same number of mice or shrews would quickly starve. It's also why cold-blooded animals do so well in the 'small size' range; heat loss is proportional to the surface area of a body, and the ratio of surface area to volume increases as body size gets smaller. So very small mammals, like shrews, have to eat virtually non-stop to generate enough body heat to keep them alive; it's bad news for a bird or mammal to be tiny. On the contrary, it's no problem for the cold-blooded amphibians and reptiles, which can be small and take life at a relatively leisurely pace. Their difficulties are of the opposite kind; the bigger you are, the longer it takes the sun to warm you up, so a frog or toad is really much better off staying small.

Distributions of the British species: telling one from t'other

Probably most people, if they think about it at all, imagine that there's just one kind of 'frog' and one 'toad' in Britain. This is understandable, because, whereas the common frog and common toad are both widespread in England, Wales and Scotland, our third species – the natterjack toad – is much rarer, and most people never come across it. Anybody who does happen to live near a natterjack colony will, however, very likely be aware of their existence; males of this species make a deafening racket with their croaks at breeding time (April and May) and can be heard up to a mile or so from their ponds – not good news for insomniacs. A distribution map of common frogs or common toads in Britain shows more or less blanket coverage, with the exception of a few offshore islands, but a map of natterjack sites is much more patchy. This toad is now found in numbers only in some coastal sand dunes of north-west England and south-west Scotland, though smaller colonies still persist in East Anglia and there is even one in southern England. All three of our native species are widespread outside Britain; common frogs and toads range right across Europe and Asia towards China, and even natterjacks can be found in a total of seventeen countries, although all of these are in Europe. It is interesting that common toads don't inhabit Ireland (perhaps St Patrick banished them with the snakes), though frogs are common there and even natterjacks can be seen in one corner. The world distribution maps shouldn't be taken too seriously; many were drawn up nearly 100 years ago by one of herpetology's folk heroes, George Boulenger, during his work at the British Museum of Natural History. This outstanding character was sent specimens from all over the world for identification, and it was largely on the basis of these that the maps were made. No doubt they are broadly correct, but any place where there was no one to collect frogs obviously won't show up on the map, whether frogs are there or not, and it's difficult to imagine places like Outer Mongolia swarming with frog collectors.

Now is a good time to explain how to identify our three native species. The pictures should help, but it's worth spelling out a few of the crucial points. Common frogs have a moist (not really slimy) skin which is quite variable in colour. Usually it is brown or grey with darker blobs, but some are more beautifully marked (particularly females, which is unusual among animals); yellowish or

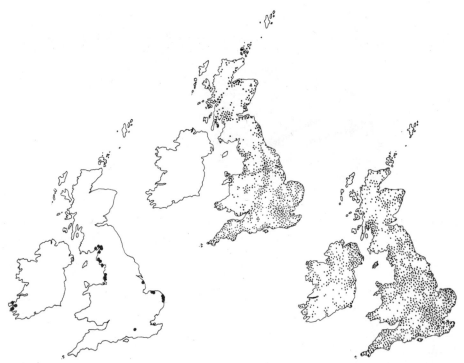

British distributions of the natterjack (left), *common toad* (centre) *and common frog* (right).

orange backgrounds with red blotches, especially around the mouth, are not uncommon. All frogs have a distinct brown patch behind each eye, which actually surrounds the eardrum and is not present in toads. Frog noses are more pointed than toad ones, and the hump in the back is more pronounced. Habits are often a useful guide, too. In summer frogs are often found in long grass, rather than under things as toads usually are, and of course leap away when disturbed. Sometimes, if alarmed, they even utter a weird shriek, and this is a dead giveaway because toads never do it. Both common and natterjack toads are plump, warty creatures with uniform brown-grey background colours (although natterjacks quite often have a greenish tinge). Common toads tend to waddle or crawl along, though they can make a few feeble hops. Natterjacks are easily identified. They have a distinct yellow line running down the middle of their back, a 100% guarantee of pure natterjack. Only two or three individuals, out of the thousands seen or handled in Britain over the years, have not had the yellow stripe. Natterjacks have much shorter back legs than common toads and often get about by running. They've even been mistaken for mice in the evening light. It's very unusual to find natterjacks anywhere other than sandy places, where they live under bits of rubbish or in little

Common toad

Common frog

Natterjack toad

burrows, often several together. Common toads also sometimes live in sand, though; habitat by itself is not a reliable guide.

Both common frogs and common toads reach similar maximum body sizes, in the region of 3½–4 inches (85–100 mm). The largest natterjacks in Britain are about 3 inches (75–80 mm) long, but most specimens of all three species are quite a bit smaller than these record holders.

Easy, isn't it? Well, you'd think so, but even naturalists make mistakes sometimes and 'authentic records' of natterjack toads are still reported occasionally from mountain tops, slag heaps and all sorts of other unlikely places. Invariably they turn out to be nonsense when checked, and they're not all accidental either. A few years ago a householder on the Isle of Wight fought a compulsory purchase order on the basis of having natterjack toads (a protected species) at the bottom of his garden. Unfortunately he hadn't done his homework; there are no records of natterjacks from the Isle of Wight and he lost his case, but I'll bet it caused a bit of head-scratching in the council offices.

Of course there are variations on the 'Mr Average' descriptions for all species. Common frogs are often at their largest and most beautifully marked in highland

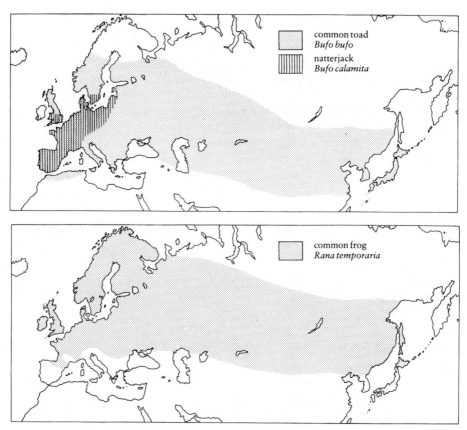

World distributions of the British species.

areas, so much so that in the early 19th century Scottish frogs were thought to be a
different species from English ones. Common toads, on the other hand, get bigger
as you go south and Italian specimens can be enormous, up to 6 inches (150 mm)
long. Probably this is because with shorter winters the animals have a longer
growing season each year, though that wouldn't explain the size of frogs in
Scotland. Another quite unexplained quirk is that common toads in China
sometimes have a yellow stripe just like our natterjack, though in all other respects
they are distinctly 'common'. Natterjacks tend to be less variable, though in Spain,
where they are particularly abundant, a lot of them have little or no yellow stripe.
Again, nobody knows why this is so.

Albino frogs are quite often found; they look creamy yellow rather than white because of lymph fluid under their skins, and in one garden near Reading there is (or was a few years ago) a population consisting mainly of this variety. White toads are much rarer, though there have been a couple of records, but none of adult natterjacks. Baby common toads sometimes have brick red markings on their warts, and some adult natterjacks (mainly females) are very attractive creatures with a green marbling effect and red tips to their warts. Who says toads are ugly?

Of course there are lots of other ways in which our three species differ from one another; these are just the most obvious, and more will be apparent as you read on. One other point is worth making here. Unlike many animals such as birds and flying insects, amphibians don't usually wander far from where they are born. So any genuine record from an area, even of a single individual, usually means that a thriving population is based close by. Formally recording frog and toad 'sightings' is therefore a particularly useful thing to do. Finding a new site for a species can be exciting, and even natterjack colonies are still being discovered occasionally. Getting them on record is, among other things, a great aid to their conservation.

The Irish Question

Ireland is renowned among naturalists for its lack of reptiles and amphibians, but St Patrick was not completely successful in keeping them out, and one species there is of particular interest. There are no common toads in the Emerald Isle, but natterjacks can be found in a few isolated spots around the south-west coast. The question is: why just this species, and only in this particular little bit of the country? They could have been introduced by man, either accidentally or on purpose, and at least one local legend does support this explanation. Ireland separated from England and Wales before the rest of Britain was isolated from mainland Europe as the sea levels rose after the last Ice Age, so this doesn't seem a very likely route for colonization. Perhaps the most probable course of events involved the formation of sand dunes along the old Ice Age coast, which used to run more or less directly between Brittany and south-west Ireland. Sand dunes are good natterjack habitat, and the toads might just have had time to move along this ancient corridor before being obliterated by the rising ocean. We will probably never know the history of Irish natterjacks for sure, but it's an interesting little aspect of distribution which should keep herpetologists arguing for many years to come.

Habitats

Wild creatures don't live just anywhere, and the sort of place in which an animal or plant can be found is called its habitat. Britain has lots of different habitats: mountains, moorlands, lowland farms, coastal sand dunes and urban gardens to name but a few. There are also more subtle but often very important distinctions to be made within these broad groups; lowland farms, for example, include tranquil pastures, woody copses, hedgerows, ponds and tracts of arable prairie among other things. How many of these are suitable for frogs and toads?

When I was a boy most people thought frogs and toads lived more or less

everywhere. Like house mice or sparrows, they were widespread and, if anything, rather too plentiful for comfort. Our garden was home to good numbers of frogs and toads, and I remember complaints about them getting under people's feet, making unsightly squashed messes and so on.

Things have changed a lot since then. On the one hand, the post-war period has seen severe declines of all three British species in many parts of the country (see p. 94), and there's no doubt that the situation is quite different now compared with the 1950s. But as well as that, and partly because of it, scientists have looked more closely at amphibian habitats and tried to find out just what it is that makes life tolerable for frogs and toads.

One feature obvious from a moment's thought is that they must be fussy in at

least one sense. This is because they need two distinctly different habitats, within fairly close reach of one another, to complete their life cycle. The first is suitable dry land, providing cover from predators, a supply of small-animal food, and a place for hibernation (see p. 55); the other is a pond to lay their eggs in and allow their tadpoles to develop. This combination is not as common as it once was.

Generally speaking, both frogs and toads are pretty adaptable creatures and can live in most of the habitats Britain has to offer. Frogs are equally at home in sand dunes around the coast and in mountains up to 1,000 metres high, as well as many of the places in between. Much the same is true of the common toad, except it's not quite so happy in sand dunes unless they are overgrown with trees or scrub. The frog is traditionally associated with pasture (remember Aesop's fable?) and the woodland edge, but it does well in open-canopy, deciduous woods, heather moors in northern England and Scotland, and in gardens everywhere. Nevertheless, there are places frogs don't like. You will be pushed to find one in heathland (too hot and dry), and they are very uncommon on chalk hills such as the Sussex Downs, and some low-lying river valleys. Countrysides like the Cambridge Fens are real no-go areas for frogs today. The pattern for the common toad is much the same, despite it being fussier than the frog in its choice of breeding pond (see p. 68). In many places the absence of frogs and toads is clearly a result of modern farming methods, particularly intensive cereal growing. Vast, hedgeless fields, blasted every year with pesticides and fertilizers and deep-ploughed are designed for just one species – the crop – and are about as hospitable as the surface of the moon to most forms of wildlife. Modern pastures, too, are often better drained than in earlier times, with cows and sheep drinking from troughs rather than the old corner ponds. These things account for the situation on the Downs and in the Fens as well as many other places, but there are areas without frogs for less obvious reasons. I know parts of the Sussex Weald where I can rely on finding newts any time, but I can be equally sure I won't see any frogs or toads. The cause of this is not known for sure, but it may be something to do with the ponds. Frogs like pools with shallow edges to lay their spawn in, preferably without fish, since these will eat most of their tadpoles. Toads go in for rather deeper ponds, and don't mind fish at all. Their tadpoles are equipped early in life with a range of poisons (see p. 82) that quickly persuade fish to leave them alone. But apart from that, frogs and toads probably choose their breeding ponds on the basis of what algae – future tadpole food – are growing in them. This in turn is probably determined by complex mixes of natural chemicals in the ponds, and it's quite on the cards that some areas (with a particular kind of clay soil, let's say) just don't provide this vital chemistry.

The situation with the natterjack is quite different. Like many British holiday-makers, this toad is most at home in the sunnier climes of Spain and the south of France. Britain is very much an outpost for natterjacks, and to survive at all here

Natterjack holidaymaker

they have to stick to the warmest places. They also need loose soil for burrowing into, so they have ended up confined to sandy coastal dunes, and the lowland heaths of southern and eastern England. These are among the hottest habitats the United Kingdom has to offer, as anyone who has walked barefoot over dry sand on a sunny day will readily agree. Natterjacks also have a liking for very shallow ponds which usually dry up altogether sometime in the summer, and not infrequently before their tadpoles have had time to grow up – thus killing the lot. They will usually choose this kind of pond even if deeper ones are available nearby, and on the face of it you might think the species has some kind of death-wish. Of course you don't actually survive for millions of years doing something totally stupid, so there must be more to it than that. Partly it's because shallow ponds get warmer than deep ones, and they also contain fewer predators (e.g. dragonfly nymphs) to kill the tadpoles. It seems that these advantages outweigh the occasional total loss of a year's offspring for this particular species.

Island life

Islands have a special fascination for biologists because odd evolutionary events can occur on them. This happens because they often get colonized by just a few species of creatures, more or less by accident, which then do much better than on the mainland where competition is more intense. Good examples are the giant tortoises of the Galapagos and other tropical islands, which have evolved to enormous sizes because there are few other grazers competing for the *vegetation. There are 'toad islands' in Europe, notably in that part of the sea which separates Denmark from southern Sweden. Some have enormous colonies of the East European green toad,* Bufo viridis, *thriving without competition from other toad species or, often, virtually anything else. Other tiny islands near the Swedish coast are inhabited just by natterjacks, which breed in rock pools regularly drenched with sea spray and live in a totally atypical stony habitat. Toad density under these circumstances can be extraordinarily high; this is the seed corn of evolution, and who can guess what might happen in places like this if left alone for a few thousand years?*

What's in a frog?

Frogs and toads are the same basic mix of bones, blood, skin, muscle, etc., as all other higher animals, but they do have a few special peculiarities. Their distinctively odd shape, for example; have you ever noticed a frog's neck? Probably not, because they don't really have one. The head seems to be stuck straight onto the shoulders, and there's no way a frog or toad can cast a backward glance except by turning right round. The rear end is equally unusual, with several backbone segments fusing together to form a long bone, the urostyle, which in turn affects the shape of the whole pelvis. This is how the frog got its hump. The skeleton has a number of less obvious oddities, too. Forearms and forelegs have only single bones rather than the two usually found in higher animals; ankle bones are long, and toe bones very long by comparison with the other bits; backbone, shoulder girdle and skull all have special features of interest to people concerned with classifying frogs and toads, or looking at their fossils; and ribs are little more than stumps, of no use at all for chest expansion. There is certainly no mistaking an anuran skeleton for any other sort of animal.

Frog skeleton

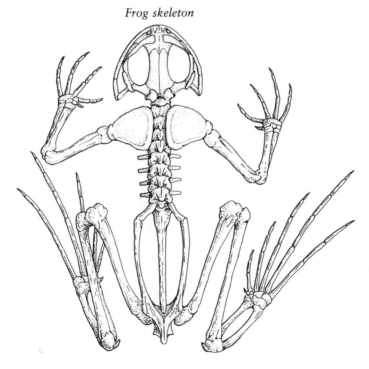

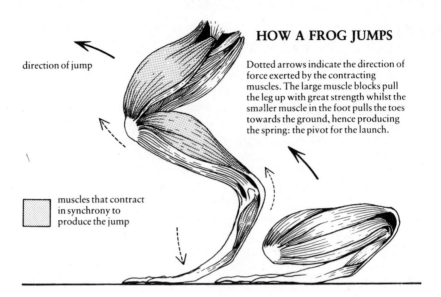

HOW A FROG JUMPS

direction of jump

Dotted arrows indicate the direction of force exerted by the contracting muscles. The large muscle blocks pull the leg up with great strength whilst the smaller muscle in the foot pulls the toes towards the ground, hence producing the spring: the pivot for the launch.

muscles that contract in synchrony to produce the jump

A frog's biggest muscles are in its back legs, for jumping or hopping. Human beings noticed them long ago, as being choice items for gourmets (see p. 110). The heart is different from ours in that it has a single main pumping chamber (ventricle) rather than the more efficient double variety; it has only a tiny volume of blood (less than 10 ml) to circulate. On the other hand, watery-looking lymph fluid is more abundant in frogs and toads than in most other creatures and there is a separate network, including mini lymph-hearts, to pump the stuff around. It is lymph fluid that gives male frogs and toads their slightly puffy appearance in spring when they are breeding.

Frogs and toads have a relatively short gut, which is quite usual in creatures that are totally carnivorous. The reason is simply that animal food is much easier to digest than plant material, and doesn't need to be kept in the body for a long time with convoluted loops of intestine. Frogs and toads vary a bit at the 'mouth' end; the British species all have tongues which are fixed at the front of the mouth, not near the back like ours. This is a great help when they go hunting (see p. 49), but some species of tropical frogs don't have any tongues at all. Teeth in frogs and toads are a bit of a joke; toads don't possess any, and frogs have what are really just a few small pegs known as 'vomerine' teeth. Since they don't have any claws either, they must be the poorest equipped predators in the business. They are also defenceless, at least in terms of biting and scratching – another bonus for anyone wanting to study them (and pretty good news for predators, too). I've never heard of frogs or toads trying to bite anyone, but I have been savaged by great crested newts on a couple of occasions. (Newts don't have serious teeth either, and it's quite a surprise to find one latching on to a finger.) At the other end, waste products and eggs or sperms all exit through the same orifice via a structure called the cloaca. From the outside there is nothing much to see in either sex, just a tiny posterior hole. Frogs and toads do have bladders, but these are really for water storage rather than excretion. A frightened toad will probably expel this water over your hand if you pick it up, but it is just water – not urine. The bulk of amphibian excretion is in solid form, including material which in higher animals appears in urine. Only a small amount is disposed of in solution, and this mainly through the skin.

Brainpower is not one of a frog's outstanding virtues. The size of the head is quite deceptive, and the space inside the skull available for brain tissue much smaller than might be imagined from the outside. Of course it does have a fully developed nervous system, including an unfortunate feature (from the frog's point of view) that has attracted the attention of scientists and teachers. The nerves to the hind legs can survive a long time after the frog has been killed, and this has made frogs popular for study – they can be stimulated in the laboratory to make the hind legs give macabre 'kicks', a procedure which has taught us a lot about how nerves work and cost an awful lot of dead frogs.

Skin is an organ of major importance to frogs and toads. Without scales, fur or feathers it's more naked than in any other group of higher animals, and plays a major role in breathing (see p. 40). Special glands keep the skin damp and supple, more so in frogs than in toads, and pigments in skin cells are crucial for camouflage and therefore the survival of the animal. The drab or blotchy colours usually blend in well with their backgrounds, making them very difficult to spot. Some patterns are still a mystery, though. Nobody knows why natterjacks have a yellow stripe, nor why some frogs have red and yellow on their bodies. Amphibian skins are not always as delicate as they look at first sight, and many contain powerful poisons to deter would-be predators. This is what the warts of toads are all about, especially the large, long ones behind the eyes, known as 'parotid glands'. Natterjacks also have small growths, called 'tubercles', on their ankles and these help them to dig

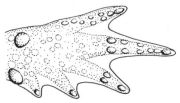

Natterjack hind foot, showing tubercles.

Left hand of common frog

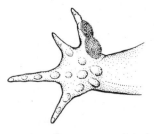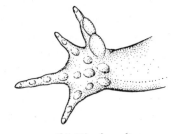

(a) Breeding — nuptial pad   (b) Non-breeding

their burrows in loose sand. And males of all three species develop swellings on some of their forefingers at breeding time, the so-called 'nuptial pads', to help them hang on to females. Often these are the best way of telling the sex of a frog or toad, because traces of them remain all year round. Male frogs and natterjack toads also have bluish or purple throats, especially at breeding time, but this guide to sex doesn't apply to common toads. Another crucial function of the skin is to take up water. Frogs and toads do not drink in the usual way, but simply absorb the water they need through their skins by sitting in a pond or puddle.

We must not forget tadpoles. These little creatures may look all head and tail, but in fact the 'head' is mostly 'body' (already there's a neck problem), packed in this case with quite a long intestine. You can often see this clearly in taddies swimming in an aquarium, because the skin on the belly is thin and almost transparent. The longer gut is needed because tadpoles eat a lot of plant food, especially algae. They have gills, of course, though these are hidden under flaps of skin after the tadpole is a few days old, and a small 'spiracle' on the side of the body to allow the water to flow out. Tadpoles (including toad ones) even have tiny teeth for scraping food off sticky surfaces. People used to think that tadpoles shed their tails when they turned into frogs, but what actually happens is that they absorb them. This very specialized process ensures that nothing is wasted – the tail essentially turns into the first food supply of the baby frog or toad.

Frogs are able to drink through their skins.

Road casualty report

The bodies of frogs and toads killed en route to their breeding ponds by road traffic can be a gruesome and depressing sight. Sometimes it's possible to reduce the casualties (see p. 7), but even if not, use can occasionally be made of the carnage. Researchers in Wales have collected the corpses of toads killed in this way to obtain valuable information about the age structure and fertility of the population. They have also been able to show, at least for the big toad colony they were studying, that road deaths were not a serious threat, however horrible the situation might appear. It is perhaps some small compensation that traffic mortality can reduce the need for any deliberate killing of animals for research purposes, and that the research itself can provide information to help conserve frogs and toads in the country as a whole.

Senses and sensibilities

A surprising thing about frogs and toads is that their senses are remarkably similar to human ones. Like us, they rely more than anything else on good eyesight and their eyes are very conspicuous, stuck on the tops of their heads. Frogs and toads don't have proper eyelids, but they do possess a transparent membrane which covers and protects the eye when underwater. The colour of the iris can be quite a distinctive feature; in common toads it is orange, while natterjacks tend to have greeny-yellow ones. Frogs and toads rely on their eyes for finding food, finding a mate and spotting potential enemies. A blind frog would have no chance of survival, although I have seen animals with only one eye that seemed to be doing alright. Frog eyes are particularly good at detecting movement, but of course we can't tell how clear a picture they see. I've certainly never been persuaded that pet frogs can distinguish their human keepers from strangers, as has sometimes been claimed. Toad eyes are especially good at night, which is when they usually go looking for food. Experiments have shown that common toads can see and catch their prey, which is always a moving target of some kind, at light intensities as low as 10 microlux. This is the equivalent of a dark night in the middle of a wood, conditions under which humans certainly can't see toads (feeding has to be recorded by the sound of the animal snapping up its victims). Even owls cannot do better than this. However, the range of vision is quite poor. Potential food creatures, being small, are not noticed if they are more than 1 foot (30 cm) or so away, although 'large' movements – like those of a human – clearly register when still several metres distant. It is purely the size of the moving object that tells a toad whether to eat it or run away from it; an interesting test is to drop a mass of wriggling worms near a toad, whose first reaction will be to run away. But then, as individual worms crawl out of the mass, the toad will turn around and start its dinner. Frogs and toads can be fooled very easily, by waving almost anything small in front of them, into having a go at it. The bait needn't be alive, or even biological – a bit of rag will do, as frog catchers in France discovered long ago (see p. 111).

Frogs have a good sense of hearing.

Hearing is also quite an important sense, especially at breeding time. Although frogs and toads do not have obvious ears, they are present and in frogs especially you can see the eardrum as a circle in the brown patch behind the eye. Males of all our species make some sort of croak during the breeding season, though natterjack toads are by far the loudest. Both sexes are attracted by these calls, which probably help guide them to particular ponds or breeding areas. Hearing must be quite acute; I remember walking towards a natterjack breeding pond one evening and passing a female walking in the same direction while we were both half a mile or so away; I didn't hear the croaking males myself until I was much nearer to them, but presumably she must have done. Probably the ears are not much used at other times of year, but in captivity some toads can be taught to associate a particular noise, such as a gentle tapping on the ground, with someone bringing food for them and quickly come out of their hiding places in anticipation.

Frogs and toads have powers of smell and taste, but we don't know as much about how they use these. Maxwell Savage carried out a lot of experiments which showed that in the spring common frogs can find their way to their breeding ponds by following a distinctive smell, borne on the wind, to its source. It turned out that this smell could even be identified as a particular chemical, glycolic acid, which is produced by algae in the ponds. There may be some very limited use of smell to help find food, too. Certainly newts, and some frogs that catch food underwater (none of our three species does this), can use smell in this way but it seems much less effective on land. Frogs and toads evidently have some kind of tasting ability; although they can be deceived into biting objects waved in front of them, anything that is not real food is promptly spat out.

Again we shouldn't forget the tadpoles, though they appear (and probably are) pretty senseless creatures. They do have eyes, and can certainly be scared by movements close to them. Watch them scatter next time you walk along the edge of a pond. They have a sense of smell, and also can probably detect vibrations from larger animals in the water or stamping along the pond bank.

Recent experiments on salamanders suggest that amphibians may have an ability to respond to the natural magnetism of the Earth, and guide their movements accordingly. Homing pigeons and a few other species have been proved to have this remarkable ability, and it may help amphibians to reach their breeding pools. It remains to be seen as to whether our own frogs and toads have this 'magnetic charm'.

Are frogs and toads intelligent? Well, toads at least do show some learning ability. Frogs are more nervous and less trainable, but of course that doesn't necessarily say anything about their brainpower – it just makes it difficult for us to measure it. Common toads can remember a wasp sting and therefore in future avoid trying to eat wasps, though they tend to forget after a week or two and the lesson has to be re-learnt. They certainly get used to people, too. Individuals vary a lot, but some get so bold as to come out and stare expectantly (for food, of course) the moment a human appears. This tameness also allows us to investigate a toad's sense of touch. In the past some authors have suggested it is cruel to handle these 'cold blooded' creatures because the heat of our hands must cause them pain, but this is patent nonsense. 'House trained' toads will climb onto a hand of their own free will if a mealworm is likely to be the reward, and often settle for quite a while with no sign of discomfort. They probably find the warmth perfectly agreeable. Even so it is better to avoid too much physical contact on account of the fear it can cause, particularly to frogs, rather than for any other reason.

Frog's eye view

Although frogs and toads rely a lot on their eyes, they don't have as good a picture of the world as we do. Some recent experiments have given us an idea of how toads cope with one of life's problems —

obstacles standing between them and their food. Like us, toads are able to appreciate the 'real' sizes of objects and gaps between them; if they are placed in front of a fence with vertical palings and with a mealworm the other side of it which they can see through the gaps, they will go either straight towards it (if the fence gaps are big enough for them to squeeze through) or round one end of the fence (if they aren't). But if the fence is quite long – 1 foot 3 inches (40 cm) or so – they will head straight for the mealworm irrespective of whether the gaps are big enough to allow them through. They can also be tricked by a double fence with a gap only in the one nearest the toad; in this situation they always go through the gap, even though they will still have to walk right round the second fence. It looks as if a toad's perception is limited to a few basic things, like making for gaps and (usually) not falling headlong into holes; but they can be deceived much more easily than people when the circumstances are not straightforward.

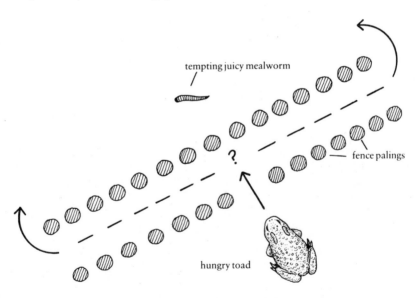

tempting juicy mealworm

?

fence palings

hungry toad

Breathing

Plants and animals need oxygen to stay alive, as any schoolchild knows. However, the whole business of breathing is more complicated in amphibians than in any other group of higher animals. This isn't really too surprising, since the lifestyle of frogs and toads involves survival in three very different media: air, land and water. Frogs and toads do not use just lungs for breathing as we and most other land animals do, although they certainly possess these organs. In addition they make use of a second and vitally important breathing surface – the skin itself, the value of which was proved by experiments many years ago which showed it to be indispensable for life both on land and in the water. Breathing entails the exchange of gases between body cells and the external environment, which in the case of frogs and toads may be either air or pondwater, depending on their activity at the time. This exchange, the uptake of oxygen and the output of carbon dioxide, goes on most efficiently through a soft wet surface in which these gases can dissolve easily. The lining of our lungs is exactly like this, but so also is the skin of a frog.

Another difference between frogs and people is that frogs have neither fully formed ribs nor a diaphragm, so amphibians cannot use the muscle and bone of

Longitudinal section through a frog's head.

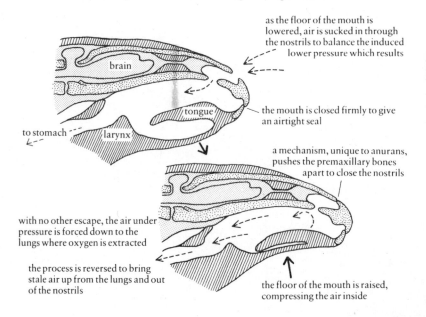

as the floor of the mouth is lowered, air is sucked in through the nostrils to balance the induced lower pressure which results

brain

tongue

the mouth is closed firmly to give an airtight seal

to stomach

larynx

a mechanism, unique to anurans, pushes the premaxillary bones apart to close the nostrils

with no other escape, the air under pressure is forced down to the lungs where oxygen is extracted

the process is reversed to bring stale air up from the lungs and out of the nostrils

the floor of the mouth is raised, compressing the air inside their chests to expand their lungs and inhale the air they need. They get round this problem by using a quite different kind of pumping system, involving their throats and special valves in their nostrils. What happens is this: a frog or toad sitting on land sucks air in through the nostrils by lowering the floor of the mouth. The nostril valves then close so the air cannot escape, and the throat pulses up and down, forcing the trapped air backwards and forwards between the lungs and mouth a few times. Finally the valves re-open, stale air is exhaled, and the cycle repeated. Anyone who has watched a frog or toad can't fail to have noticed this continuous pulsing of the throat, which speeds up if the animal is excited or alarmed. One important consequence of this rather peculiar pump mechanism is that frogs and toads cannot breathe with their mouths open. Correct working of the nostril valves is essential, and it wouldn't do for a frog to suffer from catarrh. At least one rather horrible predator of toads kills its victims partly by clogging up these vital nose passages (see p. 41). Using the lungs is therefore very important, but it was discovered many years ago that under some circumstances frogs and toads can survive for long periods without employing them at all. Undoubtedly the best example of this is when frogs hibernate in the mud at the bottom of ponds, as they very often do. For weeks or even months on end certain species, including our own common frog, can breathe quite adequately in cold water by exchanging gases through their skins alone. Hibernation is an especially good time for this because the frogs are pretty much inactive (and therefore need minimal amounts of oxygen), and because cold water carries more dissolved gases, including oxygen, than warm water does. Even so, the skin also serves as an invaluable breathing aid in summer, enabling frogs to stay submerged and hidden for several hours and even making a contribution when the animals are out on dry land. Frogs and toads are not born equal in this regard. The dry, warty toad skin is much less effective for gas exchange than the damp, supple frog skin. Toads therefore rely more heavily on their lungs than frogs do and are drowned more easily than frogs as a result. It is rare indeed for toads to attempt hibernation underwater, though under exceptional circumstances they may get away with it (see p. 57). Both frogs and toads have 'moisturizing glands' which help to keep their skins supple when away from water. This is where toads gain some advantage, their tougher and less permeable skins allowing them to survive in drier places than frogs.

Tadpoles have gills and extract oxygen from the surrounding water just like fish, but even here there is an interesting difference between common frogs and toads. Frog taddies develop lungs quite early in life, in addition to their gills, and if the pond becomes depleted of oxygen (as in hot, thundery weather) they can rise to the surface and gulp in air. Toad tadpoles don't get their lungs until they turn into toadlets, and so are less able to survive such stresses in their nursery ponds.

This complicated way of breathing has no doubt been crucial to the success of frogs and toads in their mastery of land and water habitats to an extent no other higher animals can equal. Even so, to be Jack of all Trades is still to be master of none when individual species, rather than the group as a whole, are considered. Those with the wettest, slimiest skins may look almost as at home in the water as fish – the African clawed toads (*Xenopus*) are good examples of this – but except in torrential rain these animals are quite useless on land. At the other extreme, toads like the natterjack are happy in places as dry as sand dunes but drown within an hour or so if prevented from climbing out of deep water.

Toad in a hole

There used to be a popular myth that toads can live for years entombed in a block of stone. Probably this originated with animals being found by quarrymen who didn't look too closely for holes where the toads might have crept in, but the story prompted one of the earliest ever herpetological experiments by Dean Buckland back in the 1820s. He actually walled-up living toads in cells cut in wood or stone, and then watched what happened. Of course the outcome would be obvious to any present-day naturalist, but in those times it was novel. Inevitably the toads within properly sealed cells died within a few months, but any small cracks in the walls or covers allowed the poor creatures to survive a year or two. Presumably a few insects crept in and were just enough to sustain the toads, and it's possible to imagine a tiny toad entering a natural cell through a small crack, growing too big to get out, and being trapped there for the rest of its life. Possible, but pretty unlikely, since toads usually emerge from their hiding places every night to hunt and would surely abandon a home with a small entrance when they couldn't get back in again.

Getting about

Frogs and toads are mobile creatures, but they must be considered slow coaches by comparison with most other groups of higher animals. Common toads, for instance, have three ways of getting from A to B: a kind of leisurely crawl, a rather pathetic hop, or, if in water, by swimming. But they're not particularly good at any of them. Crawling is the usual way, when hunting for food at night or migrating to breeding ponds. In summer toads generally wander no further than a few dozen yards each night, but in the spring, when heading for their breeding ponds, things get a bit more dramatic. It's not unusual for toads to travel half a mile or a mile (1–2 kilometres) at this time, all at the exhausting pace of 55–150 yards (50–150 metres) per hour. The toads seem quite exhausted by it all, usually pausing for a rest after every few steps. This sluggardliness all too often proves fatal when their routes cross busy roads, as they frequently do. Despite these disparaging remarks, toads can be very persistent. As a boy I knew a toad colony which had to surmount a vertical wooden fence about a yard high every spring; slowly, laboriously they would clamber up, taking advantage of every small crack or splinter to give them leverage. I never knew one fail to make it, some females even carrying males on their backs at the time.

If you scare a toad it will probably make a few short hops in its efforts to get away, but it all looks very ineffective and there can't be many creatures that would fail to catch a hopping toad if they wanted to. Toads rely mainly on other things for defence (see p. 58), and escape seems to be a token gesture. They can swim, of course, but are very clumsy compared with frogs and do not usually go into ponds except at breeding time and during spells of hot weather.

Natterjacks have a remarkable way of getting around: they run. Not always, of course, and they also do all the things that common toads do (except that they are even worse swimmers). But when they are hunting fast-moving prey, or when they are frightened by something, they scamper along with short but quite spectacular bursts of speed. This is a very unusual way of moving for an amphibian, and natterjacks have especially short back legs to make it more effective. In the fading light of a summer evening they are easily mistaken for mice, and where they are common have been known to cause hysteria among holidaymakers at sandy seaside resorts. Apart from helping them catch quick-moving insects, running like this is an efficient way of getting about on loose sand and this was probably an important factor in its evolution. It also produces very distinctive tracks, and one way of finding out whether natterjacks are around is to go for a walk on sand dunes early in the morning (before the sand is disturbed) and look for these tell-tale toad prints.

approx. 7–8 cm

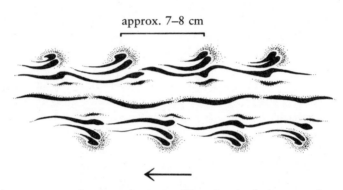

Frogs, of course, are the great hoppers. Hopping is their normal method of progression – short hops when hunting or migrating to their ponds, and great long ones when escaping from enemies. It must be admitted, though, that the British common frog is not in the big league when it comes to jumping. On a good day, with the wind behind it, one of our natives might make 24 inches (60 cm) or so – 6 or 7 body lengths. Many of the foreign competitors can do much better, and 'frogleaping competitions' are commonplace in countries like the USA and South Africa, where the local frogs put up more impressive performances. Even so, leaping is what our common frog relies on more than anything else to escape its many enemies. A few long bounds and then concealment is the usual strategy, unless water is at hand to dive into. The powerful back legs, which make for good hopping, also ensure a powerful swimming performance, much better than any toad can manage. Front legs are not used at all in swimming, they just lie back along the body to reduce drag; it's the thigh muscles, acting through the heavily-webbed 'frogman' feet, that do all the work.

It may come as a surprise to learn that frogs don't always hop, but also creep about when the mood takes them. I've seen this happen when an abundance of favourite food appears suddenly on the scene. Flying ants are a good example; frogs may then start 'stalking', almost on tiptoes: most unfroglike behaviour but obviously effective in procuring a good meal.

Adventurous types

Frogs and toads sometimes crop up in unexpected places. Cellars are a favourite hibernation site, especially for toads, if there is the smallest crack in an outside wall sufficient to let them through. At least one account exists of a cellar which acted as a toad trap; once in, the animals could not find their way out, and were forced to live there all year round. Every spring they paired up and waddled around in tandem for a while, but no spawn was ever laid. There are stories of toads being found on the tops of hedges in summer, jumping down in panic as the hedge trimmer approached; they're certainly good enough climbers for these tales to be true, but as to why they should do it . . .

Perhaps the most bizarre account is of a frog that opted out of hibernation and settled down by the fireside instead. It was told by Thomas Bell, a well known zoologist of the nineteenth century and author of the first book on British reptiles and amphibians — as reputable a source as you could wish to cite, though it must be said that his report of the story was itself a second-hand one. The animal in question is supposed to have lived in a hole in the skirting board of a house in Kingston; becoming tamer over the years, it would emerge in winter and bask on the hearth every evening nestled against the fur of the family cat. Just about everything in this yarn is contrary to what we think of as reasonable frog (or cat) behaviour, but who is to say it is completely without foundation?

Home from home

Frogs and toads cannot be said to have dens or lairs in the usual sense, but in the case of toads some of them at least do seem to show attachment to particular spots. Frogs don't often hide under things but usually tuck themselves into long grass or other vegetation, so it's difficult to know whether they stick to a specific place for very long. Toads, on the other hand, like to live under stones or other solid objects and it's quite easy to tell how long a particular animal stays in residence. Part of the folklore about toads relates to this aspect of their behaviour, with stories of individuals living in the same place for many years – more than thirty in one extreme case. I must confess to serious doubts about many of these tales, which seem particularly prone to mistakes or exaggeration. After all, one toad looks pretty much like another of the same size and what may really happen is just that a particular place is attractive to toads in general. It seems quite believable that one toad might return to the same hidey-hole every day through a single summer, but bearing in mind the long spring migrations to the breeding ponds it stretches the imagination a bit to believe the same individual comes all the way back again next year, to exactly the same spot. Experiments with toads confirm this: animals moved just a few hundred yards from where they are caught show almost no ability or inclination (whichever it is) to return home. They are far more likely to settle down happily in their new patch, and carry on as if nothing had happened.

Natterjacks live in sandy habitats and although they will creep under things if the opportunity arises, they are usually found in burrows which they dig themselves. Natterjacks are good excavators; they start work facing the sand and throwing it behind them with their front legs, and then turn round and ease themselves in with their back legs. These burrows can be 6–8 inches (15–20 cm) or so deep, and it's not unusual to find a lot of natterjacks sharing the same one. Forty-four is the highest number I have heard from a reputable source. Burrow entrances are often hidden under overhanging vegetation, but sometimes whole galleries can be seen in open, sandy banks. Frogs and toads are not at all territorial during their life on land, and are quite happy to live together in large numbers (though they're just as often found alone).

At night, frogs and toads leave their 'base camps' to go hunting. We don't know very much about the distances they cover, or whether they have favourite routes for patrolling, but by and large they don't seem to go far. Perhaps a radius of 100 yards (metres) or so from their hideout would be the usual range of a hunting trip, returning home well before dawn breaks. Needless to say it is quite difficult to actually observe any of this behaviour, but in recent years technology has arrived on this scene in a big way. Radio tracking is now the best method for following all sorts of animals about, and miniaturization has progressed to the stage where even toads can be fitted with tiny transmitters (2 or 3 g in weight). The main problem is in making sure that transmitter and toad don't part company, and all sorts of harnesses have been designed to do this. It's even possible to persuade toads to swallow their transmitters, and then follow them for a day or two until they pass out the other end. None of this causes the animal any harm, nor apparently alters its behaviour in any detectable way. Individuals can be followed at night using a receiver made up from an old car radio, with suitable aerial, and it helps to mark the harness with a blob of luminous paint for close-up identification. It's all very expensive though (especially when a frog disappears with your transmitter), and there's a lot of paperwork involved. The BBC is keen to ensure that no 'radio frog' takes to the air on the same wavelength as the 9 o'clock news and so you must obtain a licence. So far radio tracking of amphibians is still in its infancy, and there aren't many results to talk about. Some animals have been followed, but have only done predictable things: walk about, eat a few insects, and go home. This kind of work should prove very interesting at migration time, and also in telling us about hibernation sites, but that is all for the future.

Frogs and toads are not always as parochial as this story makes out. Sometimes, even in summer, they travel much longer distances and set themselves up in a new home a mile or more away from their starting place. We know almost nothing about the 'whys', 'wherefores' and 'how oftens' of this; we just know that some individuals do do it, perhaps the tramps of the frog and toad world. It's the reason why, just occasionally, somebody finds a toad miles from the nearest pond in what appears to be a quite unsuitable habitat. Presumably this habit sometimes pays off, because if a new pond is created somewhere these characters will be the first to benefit from it.

Dining out

Frogs and toads are hunters, and vegetables are not part of their diet. Every night in summer they set out to stalk their prey among the myriad of small creatures that swarm about their habitats. They are just as happy to eat during the daytime if anything comes their way, but it's too dangerous to wander about looking for food before darkness falls. What frogs and toads look for is movement, the sure sign of a meaty meal 'on the hoof'. Frogs, being agile, can jump up at insects flying by with a

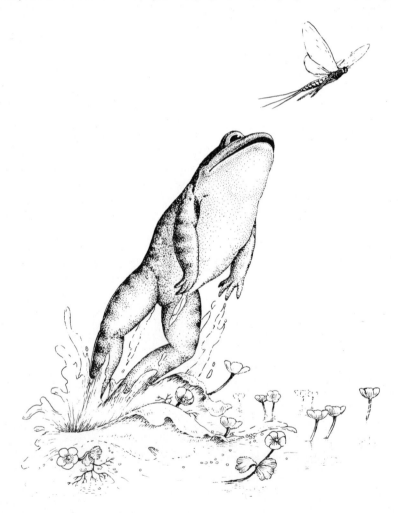

fair chance of catching them, and natterjacks can run after scurrying beetles. Mostly, though, eating is a more leisurely affair. If some small, creeping beast is caught sight of, the frog or toad immediately becomes visibly excited; the whole body cranes over towards it, the toes twitch with nervous anticipation. Seconds pass (it can seem like hours if you're watching this performance), there's a sudden 'blip', and it's all over. What has happened is too quick for the human eye to follow: the mouth opens and the tongue, hinged at the front, is flicked out at the unsuspecting dinner. Fully extended to half an inch (15 mm) or so, the sticky end of the tongue makes contact and transfers the unfortunate creature straight back to the waiting mouth – all in much less than a second. Once inside there's no chance of escape, and the prey is swallowed whole – sometimes with assistance from the eyes, of all things, which retract back into the head in a kind of 'blink' during the swallow.

Not all attacks are successful, though, and quite often the potential meal gets away. Sometimes this is just bad shooting, but toads especially have a habit of waiting for what seems like ages before striking slow-moving prey. It's infuriating to watch a worm finally disappear down its hole just as the toad decides to have a go at it; presumably it must be even more annoying for the toad. Relatively large prey, like worms, sometimes hang out of the mouth and thrash about for a while before being swallowed, making for a truly gruesome spectacle. Bits of worm are

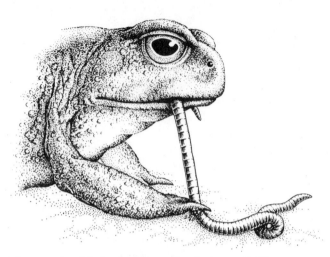

stuffed into the mouth with the forelegs, often being pulled between a couple of toes to remove sticking dirt and rubbish. The appetites of frogs and toads are gargantuan, and seem to know no bounds. There appears to be little feeling of satiation, and many individuals will continue to eat for as long as food is offered. This has even been known to result in worms being passed out alive at the other end, when the digestive system could no longer cope with more food. On the other hand, frogs and toads can go a long time without any food at all if circumstances force this upon them. No eating goes on during hibernation, and common frogs and toads don't feed while breeding either, so there is an effective fast from November through to April. Even in summer starvation for several weeks seems to do no irreversible harm, a rapid recovery following the reappearance of a food supply. Feeding time is just about the only occasion outside the breeding season when frogs and toads get emotional towards each other. Usually they cohabit perfectly peacefully, but everything changes when food appears. Any toad that is successful in catching a passing insect is likely to be subjected to a barrage of tongue flicks from his frustrated neighbour – though these don't inflict any physical damage.

People have tried to find out what frogs and toads eat in the wild, as opposed to just watching them in captivity. The best method for doing this is quite a new one, involving a stomach 'pump' which disgorges the contents without harming the animal at all. Even so, it's not work for the impatient – poring over sample after sample under the microscope, trying to identify bits of beetles, flies, etc. At first sight it looks as if frogs and toads simply eat everything they come across that moves and is small enough to swallow. However, there is a bit more to it than that. The frog's menu has a high content of slugs and snails, probably because these tend (like frogs) to live in dampish places. When counting items in a series of frog

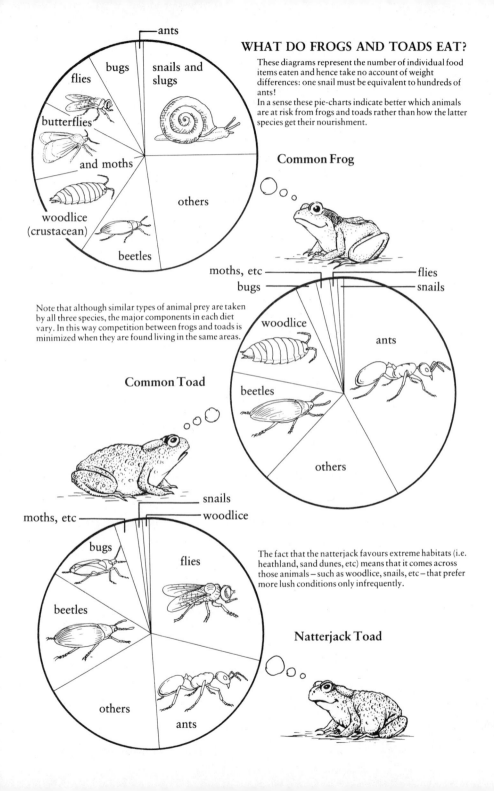

WHAT DO FROGS AND TOADS EAT?

These diagrams represent the number of individual food items eaten and hence take no account of weight differences: one snail must be equivalent to hundreds of ants!

In a sense these pie-charts indicate better which animals are at risk from frogs and toads rather than how the latter species get their nourishment.

Common Frog

(pie-chart labels: ants, snails and slugs, bugs, flies, butterflies, and moths, woodlice (crustacean), beetles, others)

Note that although similar types of animal prey are taken by all three species, the major components in each diet vary. In this way competition between frogs and toads is minimized when they are found living in the same areas.

Common Toad

(pie-chart labels: moths, etc, bugs, flies, snails, woodlice, ants, beetles, others)

Natterjack Toad

(pie-chart labels: moths, etc, snails, woodlice, bugs, flies, beetles, others, ants)

The fact that the natterjack favours extreme habitats (i.e. heathland, sand dunes, etc) means that it comes across those animals – such as woodlice, snails, etc – that prefer more lush conditions only infrequently.

stomachs, 25% or more will usually turn out to be those molluscs. Since they are also some of the biggest things frogs eat, it is obvious that they constitute an important part of the diet; individual frogs have been found with more than 10 snails in their bellies. Snail shells are no problem for the frog's digestive system – calcium carbonate dissolves easily in stomach acid, very much like indigestion tablets. Common toads and natterjacks live in drier places and eat far more insects, especially beetles and ants. In terms of numbers it's common to find more than 40% of the animals in a toad's stomach are ants, and more than 15% are beetles; but ants are tiny, so it is probably beetles that provide most of the 'meat' in a toad's diet. Natterjacks are just a little bit different, one study showing fly larvae (especially cranefly ones) made up 29% of the numbers and 34% of the weight of food items collected over a full summer. Beetles were also important, and most of the differences must just stem from hunting in different habitats, which in turn contain different types of prey. Minor contributors to frog and toad banquets include earthworms, spiders, millipedes, centipedes, woodlice, flies, moths, butterflies, caddis flies, earwigs, bugs and springtails. In southern Europe, scorpions can be added to the list. It doesn't take more than a glance to see that this is very good news for gardeners, and there is every reason to encourage frogs and toads in suburban habitats (see p. 98).

Despite this extensive menu, some creatures are avoided. Hairy caterpillars, for example, are usually rejected because of the poison in their spines, and it is very unusual for a frog or toad to hunt wasps. Bees, on the other hand, are more commonly taken – perhaps because they can only sting once, whereas wasps can keep at it and cause a lot of discomfort. Feeding habits seem to be highly individual; I have known some toads take bees readily, others show no interest in them, and some apparently learn to avoid them for a while after being stung in the mouth. There have been reports, which I can well believe, of toads taking up residence outside beehives and snapping up workers on their way home. Entomologists have had similar experiences around their moth traps at night, and toads seem to be quite cute in this regard, gobbling up insects attracted to the light.

Unlike their parents, tadpoles are not quite such greedy predators. They are omnivorous, and can live and grow exclusively on plants if necessary. In the wild, algae and single-celled animals ('protozoa') are their main source of nourishment and they spend much of their time grubbing around water plants or in pond mud for these microscopic organisms. They need a lot to grow properly, and food passes right through a tadpole gut in four hours or so. They are the 'grazing animals' of the pond bottom. However, taddies are not always so innocent; dead animals that happen to be in the pond (including their own parents) are rapidly devoured, and so are batches of frog and toad spawn laid later than the rest, or even their sick or injured brethren. In captivity tadpoles thrive on boiled lettuce or, simplest of all, the pellet food sold by petshops for rabbits and hamsters. Only when they metamorphose into tiny froglets or toadlets do they become exclusively carnivorous, as miniature versions of their parents.

Big game hunters

Frogs and toads are quite good at judging the sizes of objects, and this applies particularly well to potential prey. It's obviously important; mistaking a snake for a large worm could be fatal. So bigger frogs and toads tend to eat bigger prey, and the diet of the largest species can include warm-blooded creatures. Marine toads (see p. 108), and even the large common toads found in southern Europe, have no difficulty devouring baby mice, and may often do so. Our native British species are too small to devour this kind of thing but the introduced marsh frog is quite big enough, and has been accused of eating mice, fish up to 3 inches (75

mm) long, and even nestling birds. I don't doubt that these things are possible in captivity, but as marsh frogs normally spend their entire lives in or next to water it seems unlikely that mice or birds often fall into their mouths. Small fish, on the other hand, may well have a rough time.

One result of the way a toad sees the world is that snakes don't always have the last laugh when they meet one. A small snake will indeed be mistaken for a worm and readily attacked. Even baby adders have been seen disappearing into a toad's mouth — a classic case of the biter bit.

Hibernation

Frogs and toads certainly disappear somewhere in the winter, although strictly speaking they don't really hibernate. This term is now used formally by biologists for those animals, like hedgehogs and dormice, that experience a major change of metabolism at this time. Even so, hibernation is such a popular and well known term that I, and many others, still tend to use it pretty indiscriminately for frogs and toads just as much as for other animals. Some mammals and reptiles virtually go into a 'trance', and once in it stay that way until spring. Spells of unusually warm weather in late autumn or winter leave many of these hibernators quite unmoved, and they stay in their comatose condition more or less come-what-may. It's a great advantage for small mammals to be able to do this, because they would need a lot of

THE ANURAN YEAR

JANUARY	FEBRUARY	MARCH	APRIL
Hibernating, but wake for short spells if the temperature rises.	Many still hibernating, but frogs tend to move off to their breeding ponds.	Early March: toads migrate *en masse* to breeding ponds and frogs spawn. Late March: toads spawn, some natterjacks migrate, and some frog tadpoles hatch.	Natterjacks spawn. Frog and toad tadpoles hatch and grow. Adult toads leave the ponds.
MAY	JUNE	JULY	AUGUST
Natterjacks continue to spawn. Metamorphosis of early frog and some toad tadpoles. Adult frogs leave the ponds.	Young frog- and toadlets leave the ponds. A few natterjacks still spawning.	Adult frogs live in long grass. Remaining natterjack tadpoles undergo metamorphosis and any remaining froglets leave the water.	Late natterjack toadlets leave the water.
SEPTEMBER	OCTOBER	NOVEMBER	DECEMBER
All young animals eat greedily to gain body reserves for winter.	Hibernation begins as the weather becomes cooler, male frogs under water and all others on land.	Hibernating, but wake occasionally. Some young animals may still be hunting. Natterjacks burrow into sand or use existing holes.	Hibernating, but wake to feed in warm weather for short periods.

food to maintain their normal summer temperatures and this just isn't around in winter, whether or not there are any mild spells. Being 'cold blooded', frogs and toads need much less food than warm-blooded creatures anyway so the problem is not as severe for them. However, since they can't generate their own body heat, the falling temperatures of autumn force them to become less active and to take some refuge from severe cold and frost. They do not enter any special physiological state, and any mild weather is likely to generate some amphibian activity, including a little hunting; frogs have been caught with food in their stomachs under such circumstances. For most of the time, though, they are more or less torpid.

As soon as the night temperature drops towards freezing point, usually sometime in October, frogs and toads start to seek out their winter quarters. In the case of frogs this can be under old logs, in stone walls, compost heaps, or quite often at the bottom of a pond. Sometimes, but not always, this is the pond they will use for spawning the following spring. Overwintering underwater seems to be largely a male preserve; females and immature frogs mostly stay somewhere on land. The special properties of frog skin allow the animals to 'stay under' for long periods during the winter (see p. 41), and ice on top of a pond is not usually a danger to them. However, they do suffer in exceptionally cold winters. A few years ago reports came in from all over the country of frogs found dead in ponds when the ice melted after a particularly long freeze, and there is no doubt they cannot survive actually being frozen solid in ice. Most deaths, though, are probably due to suffocation. At the bottom of the pond frogs can usually stay clear of the ice itself,

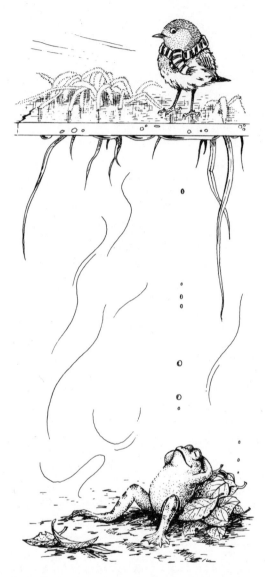

but the oxygen levels in the water gradually drop as last autumn's dead plants rot away, and no fresh oxygen can enter through the frozen surface. Poisonous gases such as hydrogen sulphide, and other undesirables like carbon dioxide build up and these may prove too much for frogs and fish in a severe winter. In most years, though, the bottom of a pond is undoubtedly a good place to be. Temperatures stay more constant than on land, and you're less likely to be found by a rummaging predator. Even so, frogs don't always show much sense in their choice of pond. Some years back I made a very shallow pool in my garden, nowhere more than 3 inches (75 mm) deep, for rearing natterjack tadpoles. The following autumn frogs piled into it in ridiculous numbers – at one stage I was removing 30 – 40 per day – obviously intending to overwinter there, despite the fact that being so shallow it was virtually certain to freeze solid (which in fact it did, on several occasions) and kill them all. Fortunately my efforts were enough to keep them out, but I subsequently had to abandon the pond rather than face the prospect of some future frog mass suicide.

Toads almost always overwinter on land, in some secluded place like a hole in the ground or under a pile of stones. It's surprising how even quite a thin layer of soil or debris protects against frosts, except of course in a very severe winter, and lots of animals make use of this kind of situation. Many toads may hole up together in a particularly good 'hibernaculum', from which they will all set out in spring to their breeding ponds. These hibernacula are rarely found except by accident, and may contain other animals besides toads. Newts, lizards and even snakes – which in summer might well eat the toads – declare a truce for this battle against the elements. One effect of the cold is to make toads go very dark in colour, and animals caught out on a cold night can look almost black. Very rarely, toads may hibernate underwater like frogs. This has been recorded occasionally in Britain, and in Sweden large numbers of common toads have been seen sitting on the bottom of fast-flowing rivers in winter.

Natterjacks always hibernate on land, deep in soft sand. This may be in their own burrows, or in those dug by other animals. They have been seen climbing up sandy banks to enter sand martin holes, and in Germany natterjacks have been recorded 3 yards (metres) below ground level in winter. In England they rarely go one tenth of that depth, probably because our winters are generally less severe.

Poison

On the face of it, frogs and toads look like ideal food for a host of carnivorous creatures: soft, meaty and not all that good at moving fast to escape pursuit. And this is in fact true of frogs, which have little to defend them apart from fleetness of hop. Toads, however, have a more subtle armoury at their command. The major function of the warts on a toad's back is to produce and, when necessary, secrete a range of substances which vary from being mildly unpleasant to the taste to downright dangerous poisons. Large amounts of these toxins are made by the so-called parotid glands, the long raised 'lumps' which extend backwards behind each eye.

Now, toads are fairly placid sorts of creatures and they don't start squirting these poisons around unless they feel very threatened indeed. Just picking up a toad will never panic it enough to secrete its poisons, and they are remarkably indifferent even to quite rough handling (as all too many schoolchildren could testify). So holding a toad is quite harmless; the most that is likely to happen is that it will empty its cloacal bladder (a clear, watery fluid with no poisons in it) onto your hand, and you may detect just a faint smell characteristic of the species in question. Natterjacks, for example, are supposed to smell of gunpowder or 'burnt india rubber', which sounds disgusting but in my experience is usually too faint to be noticed.

What really upsets a toad is severe pressure, such as being accidentally trodden on or, worse, being seized in the jaws of some animal. It is not uncommon for inexperienced dogs or cats to 'have a go' at a toad, and the reaction is usually quick and effective. A white, sticky substance appears on the toad's skin and its would-be predator responds more or less immediately by salivating, frothing at the mouth, snorting and trying to wipe the stuff off as fast as possible. Sometimes there is even a localized paralysis. Needless to say, the toad is promptly dropped and forgotten. If the attacker gets a big dose of the poison it is quite likely to vomit, and show signs of general discomfort for some time afterwards, but nothing more serious normally follows. It's a good lesson, and rarely needs to be re-learnt.

The question arises as to how effective these toxins are against natural predators. Toads are drab creatures, relying on camouflage rather than the bright warning colours displayed by some of the very poisonous arrow-poison frogs (see p. 16), and this suggests that their toxins must be less than foolproof. It turns out that some creatures have indeed learnt how to kill and eat the insides of toads, leaving the poisonous skins uneaten and useless (see p. 64). Grass snakes are important predators of amphibians and always swallow their prey whole – they don't have the option of leaving the skin – and it has been found that individual snakes vary in their attitude to toads. Some do ignore them, but others eat them readily and are unaffected by the poisons. Toads clearly don't have things all their own way, but it does seem likely that they suffer less predation than frogs as a result of their chemical defences.

Quite a bit is known about the chemistry of toad poisons and their effectiveness under laboratory conditions. At least four kinds of active substances are involved:

Biogenic amines are compounds related to adrenalin; they have a number of effects, such as causing constriction of blood vessels and sometimes muscular spasms.

Alkaloids are a well-known group of poisons and include those produced by deadly nightshade and some other dangerous plants. There are some special toad alkaloids including 'bufotenine' and 'bufotenidine', and these too cause constriction of blood vessels and thus the raising of blood pressure. One of them (O'-methyl bufotenine) is even a potent hallucinogen.

Steroids are a very widespread group of chemicals, including many well known hormones (estrogens, in 'the pill'). A feature of steroids is that very small amounts can have dramatic effects, and toad steroids (bufogenins) act as strong local anaesthetics.

Steroid esters are derived from steroids, and include the so-called bufotoxins.

With this combination it isn't too surprising that toad skin is not a popular meal. Lab tests have shown that, in the 'sliding scale' of toxic substances, bufotoxins are about as poisonous as strychnine and curare and twenty times more dangerous than cyanide. Cobra venom, however, is over a thousand times more lethal than anything a toad can produce and the most toxic substances known – produced by bacteria causing botulism food poisoning – are ten thousand times more dangerous still. Many of these compounds have the added advantage (or disadvantage, depending how you look at it) of direct access to the bloodstream, whereas toad poisons are of course taken by mouth and therefore considerably less effective. I've never heard of any animal dying after an encounter with a British toad. The most serious consequences seem to ensue when one amphibian swallows another. There are now several instances on record of north American bullfrogs eating European fire salamanders in captivity, and dying shortly afterwards from a very acute form of food poisoning. Fire salamanders are equipped with a poison apparatus similar to that found in toads.

Newt tasting

In their new-found enthusiasm for natural history and science, the Victorians keenly investigated every novelty that came their way. A classic example of this was the tasting of amphibian poisons by one Miss Ormerod, determined to find out for herself just what it was like trying to eat (in this case) a great crested newt. These newts, like toads, produce defensive poisons from warts on their skin. What she actually did was to bite a newt very gently, just enough to make it respond. The results were evidently most unpleasant, and are best described in her own words: 'The first effect was a bitter astringent feel in the mouth, with irritation of the upper part of the throat, numbing of the teeth . . . and in about a minute a strong flow of clear saliva. This was accompanied by much foam and violent spasmodic action, approaching convulsions . . . The experiment was followed by headaches lasting for some hours, general discomfort . . . and slight shivering fits.' In the light of this description it shouldn't be necessary to stress that any attempt to repeat this kind of thing would be most foolhardy. Toad poisons are now known to be even more powerful than crested newt ones.

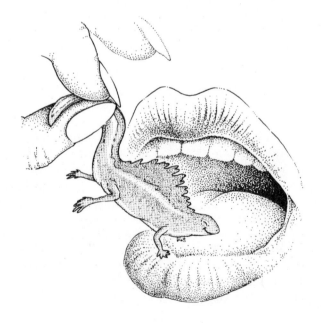

Predators and life expectancy

Now seems a good time to ask some rather basic questions about frogs and toads: for instance, how long do they live, and how many of them survive to a ripe old age? What animals eat them, and how far do these predators rely on frogs and toads to make a living? To try and answer questions like this we have to look at a chart of 'births' and 'deaths', and then try to figure out what goes on in between. So the first thing we can do is count how many eggs frogs and toads lay each year, a subject about which there is now quite a lot of information. Frogs and toads seem to keep on growing for several years after they reach maturity – indeed they may never stop growing, but we're still not quite sure about that – so older means bigger, and bigger also means more eggs. Tim Halliday found that a small female common toad may only lay about 800 eggs, whereas a large one could manage 2,600. Common frogs often lay between 1,500 and 3,000, and natterjack toads anything from 1,500 to more than 6,000. Precious few of these will ever get to be baby frogs or toads, let alone adults. Indeed, some will not even hatch because they are killed by ice or spawn fungus, or eaten by predators (see p. 80), or may not have been properly fertilized. An enormous variety of creatures make a meal out of tadpoles, especially the very small ones in their first two weeks of life (see p. 81). By the time metamorphosis comes, no more than 1–5% of the originals will still be alive; in many ponds it will be 0%, especially for natterjacks which so often lay in puddles and other daft places. Natterjacks make up for this in 'good' years when circumstances conspire to be just right; then, more than 50% survival to toadlet can sometimes happen and the ground is covered in baby natterjacks. Success for this species is probably much more erratic than for the other two, but over a period of years things obviously balance out to be much the same.

Problems certainly don't end at the froglet or toadlet stage. In the 2–3 years before sexual maturity, another 95% or so of the toadlets will probably die or be killed – 95% of that pitiful 1–5%. So of an original (say) 2,000 eggs, probably less than 5 will live long enough to come back and spawn. If a frog or toad does survive to become an adult its life is then relatively safe, though still far from easy. In captivity common frogs have been kept for 12 years, common toads exceptionally for about 20, and natterjacks for about 15. Generally speaking 10–15 would be a very ripe old age, but it's rare indeed to find a specimen in the wild that has survived anything like that length of time. How do we know that? A fascinating recent discovery has been that frog and toad bones have 'growth rings' just as trees do, with a new one being laid down every year when the animal goes into hibernation.

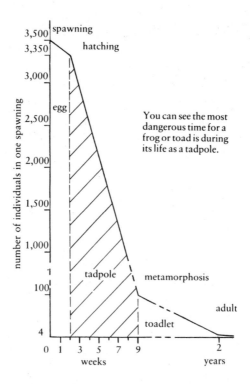

Graph showing the average mortality rate for the natterjack toad (others fairly similar).

It's possible to age a frog just by clipping off the end of a single toe (this does no harm if carried out carefully) and looking at a section under the microscope. When you do this, you find few frogs as old as 7 or 8; some common toads and natterjacks may live to be 10 or 11 but most of all three species die much younger, within the first 3 or 4 years of adulthood. On average, it can be worked out that about half the toads alive one year will be dead by the next; there is thus about a 50% 'survivorship' from year to year. This may sound a horrifyingly low survival rate, but it depends very much what you compare it with as to how nasty it seems. The life expectancy of a frog or toad is much better than that of mammals of similar size, like shrews or mice, or many of the small songbirds. Most of these warm-blooded 'advanced' types are lucky indeed to survive more than a year or so, and a mouse will die of old age at 3. Their advantage, of course, is that juvenile mortality is much lower and a far higher proportion of baby mice get to be adults than tadpoles get to be frogs.

So what is killing off half the frogs and toads each year? The list of predators, especially for frogs, is a long one and we still have little idea which are the most important. Among the animals we know eat them are pike, grass snakes, seagulls, herons, owls, crows, weasels, stoats, otters, rats, hedgehogs, foxes and domestic cats. Of these, grass snakes are the only ones that 'specialize' in frogs, the others merely include them in a more varied diet. This specialization by snakes has led to a dramatic response in the behaviour of toads. When approached by a snake, toads become very frightened indeed, inflating themselves with air and stretching up on tip-toes in the so-called 'defence posture'. The point of this is very simple: snakes have a good idea of how big an object they can swallow, so if a toad can make itself

Defence position of toad when confronted by a grass snake.

look larger, it might just fool the snake into leaving it alone. Frogs don't do this but leap or swim rapidly away; grass snakes, however, are proficient swimmers themselves and think nothing of diving into a pond in pursuit of their dinner. It's an art they learn young too, because several naturalists have reported watching baby grass snakes hunting tadpoles in ponds during the spring. The breeding season is a particularly dangerous time, and every year the frogs visiting my garden pond to spawn take a bashing from the local carnivores. Most of this goes on at night, and a couple of years ago an especially severe series of attacks was leaving the lawn a gruesome battleground every morning. I eventually stayed up to find out what was going on; the culprit turned out to be a magnificent dog fox, whom I deterred by erecting a temporary fence around the pond until breeding was over.

Quite a few animals will attack toads, learning to rip them open and just eating the insides without the poisonous skin. I have seen lots of natterjacks treated like this and left in neat rows around their breeding ponds, a distasteful habit for which seagulls seem to be responsible. But it may be the killers that leave no trace at all that are the most serious. Grass snakes come into this category, and so do hedgehogs which I have watched consume whole frogs in less than a minute. The trouble with predation (for scientists) is the difficulty of studying it, and most of what we know amounts to a list of odd observations made by many people in many different places. It's still impossible to answer the simple question: what is the most important predator of frogs and toads?

Parasites, disease and the dreaded fly

Very little is known about frog diseases and parasites. There is a kind of white, stringy fungus which infects spawn and can kill a lot of eggs if the weather is unusually cold; and people who dissect frogs and toads sometimes find flukes and worms of various kinds, especially nematodes, in their stomachs and intestines. It is usually impossible, though, to guess how much they affected the life of the animal. One group of parasites, called 'Polystoma' worms, live in frogs' bladders and manage to produce their eggs to coincide exactly with the breeding season of their hosts. These hatch in the pond and infect new tadpoles, a most effective way of propagating into the next frog generation. These worms don't seem to do the frogs any harm, but the same cannot be said of some nasty bacterial infections such as 'red leg'. Diseases of this type can devastate colonies of captive frogs, but this is probably because they are living under unnaturally crowded conditions. It's rare to see an infected wild frog, and I doubt whether bacteria are much of a problem under natural circumstances.

There is one very unpleasant beast which specifically attacks common toads. It's always fatal, and strictly speaking is a predator rather than an infection or a parasite. This is the 'toad fly', a greenbottle, Lucilia bufonivora. It's quite small enough to be eaten by a toad, and probably is sometimes, because during the summer female flies go looking for toads to lay their eggs on. These hatch on the doomed animal's back, and the maggots crawl upwards into the nostrils and around the eyes. Blocking the nose is a good way of suffocating a toad (see p. 65), and stricken animals crawl about 'clucking' – opening and shutting their mouths in vain attempts to breathe. Once inside the toad, the maggots just start eating; the wretched animal soon dies, and is devoured completely except for the bones and skin. In due course the fly maggots turn into pupae, still inside the corpse, and then into new adult flies. Apparently these insects are quite common, but fortunately seeing a victim of them is not, and we don't really know how many toads they account for. It could be quite a few; one study in Holland found fly eggs on 8% of the toads caught over a period of two summers.

Migration

Frogs and toads are at their most active in the spring, and this is when they are usually seen. Spring is their breeding season, and it starts with an especially dramatic event – migration to the spawning ponds. Very often frogs and toads return to the same pond year after year, and this is usually the one in which they were born. Toads are especially fastidious about this, but frogs can be more easily persuaded to try somewhere new; this is best seen in the speed with which new garden ponds are colonized by local frogs, which evidently aren't concerned about returning to their old nursery site.

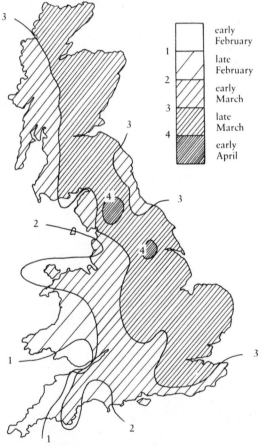

Contour map of Britain, showing periods during which first frog spawning is recorded (after A. Cooke).

Frogs are first off the mark in migrating, though their efforts are generally less spectacular than those of toads. This is because quite a few of them, especially the males, hibernate in their breeding ponds and so don't have any migrating to do. Most of the females and some of the males will have to make a journey, though, and for herpetologists this eagerly anticipated event marks the start of the new spring. It begins early, long before the first cuckoo is heard and usually before the daffodils are in bloom. Exactly when will depend not only on the weather, but also the part of the country. Frogs won't travel on cold or frosty nights, and mild conditions with at least a touch of rain in the air seem ideal. In Cornwall, frogs will be on their way in January, or even late December under exceptional circumstances – stretching it a bit to call this a spring affair. Further north or east, frogs 'sleep in' longer and the last ones to make their treks are those in eastern England (mid – late March) or in the high mountains such as the Lake District (as late as early April in some years). The exact cause of this variation has been the subject of much research and debate, but it looks as if the milder the winters normally experienced by an area, the earlier the frogs will start their breeding activities. Before the last war, the Meteorological Office collected records of 'first frog spawn seen' from all over the country for a number of years, and Maxwell Savage later carried out a detailed analysis of the data to try and get to the bottom of the problem. He ended up with the suggestion that the frogs are responding to the amounts of algae (microscopic, single-celled plants) present in their prospective breeding pools; the climate is acting indirectly, by helping or hindering the growth of these algae rather than influencing the frogs themselves. This explanation makes a lot of sense because tadpoles feed mainly on algae, and if frogs have a way of telling when the crop is 'ripening' it would inform them both when to breed, and also which particular ponds to choose.

Frogs certainly seem to know where they're going, and how to get there, at migration time. They won't go to just any old pond, and there are many tales of them moving through an apparently perfect pool (to the human eye) en route to the one in which they will eventually spawn. They only travel at night, so you will need determination (and a torch) to see them at it. Some other features also seem to fit with the 'algae hypothesis'; frogs tend to move upwind, as if reacting to a smell being carried towards them, and algae are known to have very distinctive odours. Also, migration and spawning may occur two or three weeks earlier in one pond than in another quite close by; perhaps the algae in the later ponds are taking longer to grow dense enough for the frogs to smell them.

Another reason that frog migration is less spectacular than that of toads is because frogs tend to travel in several minor 'waves' rather than one big rush. I can watch frogs coming in my garden in dribs and drabs on suitable nights from the end of January right through February, gradually accumulating in the ponds but not usually spawning before the first week of March.

Toads do things a bit differently. They usually start later than frogs, sometimes several weeks later; in Sussex, where I live, frogs most often breed in the first week of March and toads in the third or fourth week, though this can of course be affected by the weather in any particular year. Toads seem quite happy to migrate on dry nights as long as it's at least a few degrees above freezing, and it's not uncommon for them to move in daytime as well. This, coupled with their tendency to move *en masse* (an entire colony will migrate to its breeding pond within a few days), and the generally longer distances toads travel (up to a mile, or 1–2 km) at this time, make it an altogether more dramatic affair than the frogs' performance. The longer distances are probably necessary because toads are much fussier than frogs about which ponds they will breed in; there may be as many as 5 or 6 'frog' ponds for every 'toad' pond in an area, though we still don't know the reason for this. It's likely that toads also use a sense of smell to reach their chosen pond, and animals deliberately moved away from their breeding sites have shown a strong ability to return 'home', so long as the distances are not too great. The determination of marching toads at this time of year is quite remarkable; all sorts of impassable-looking obstacles, including walls, are tackled wherever they get in the way. Moving in daytime makes them more vulnerable than usual to predators, and crows in particular often kill quite a few during the migration days. If a male toad meets a female during this trek, he immediately jumps on her back and she will have to carry him the rest of the way to the pond, no matter how far it is or what barriers still have to be surmounted. In fact, the great majority of female toads are already 'lumbered' like this when they reach their ponds, another difference from the frog situation.

There are lots of unexplained things about toad migrations even now. I saw a good example of this a few years ago, when one of my local toad ponds was emptied for repair just before the toads were due to arrive. The result was that some 80 female toads turned up and sat on the dry pond bottom, looking suitably perplexed. Not only do we have to explain how these toads found their way (there was obviously nothing to smell), but also why only 6 males turned up. Next year the pond was full again and all the toads, of both sexes, were back as usual. There are other stories of toads continuing to migrate to pond sites several years after the pond had been filled in, which indicates that memory must play some part.

Natterjacks also migrate to their breeding ponds, but not as spectacularly as common toads. They tend to be more like frogs, travelling mainly at night and arriving in small groups over a long period of time. Their breeding season is later still, starting sometime in April in most places.

You may think that none of this is in the same league as the birds and insects, some of which travel thousands of kilometres each year using sophisticated navigation systems involving the sun, stars, and the Earth's magnetic field. But for

Toads will pass all obstacles to get to their breeding ponds.

the small, relatively immobile frogs and toads the spring migration represents a considerable achievement – and they're a darned sight easier to follow than swallows to Africa.

Toads on roads

The annual carnage of toads migrating to their breeding ponds, run over by traffic on roads they have to cross, has not been ignored by naturalists and conservationists. 'Toads on roads' campaigns of various sorts have been tried in Britain and elsewhere, and usually at least one rescue operation features on the TV each spring. Several remedies have been attempted. The simplest involves a team of volunteers manning the point where toads cross the road for the several days and nights of peak migration, collecting them up as they arrive and carrying them to the other side. Some places even have special road signs depicting a toad, unfolded at the key time, warning drivers to motor carefully over the coming section of road. More elaborate ideas include toad 'tunnels' under the roads, rather like those provided for badgers on some motorways; the design has to be just right before toads will use them, though, and they are expensive to install. Another idea is to put a toad-proof fence parallel to the road, with buckets set into the ground at intervals along it. Toads coming to the fence wander along trying to get round, fall into a bucket and are collected for carriage across the road early each day.

All of these methods can work fairly well, but it's much more difficult helping the toads get back again when they have finished breeding because they leave the pond area in dribs and drabs over a long period of time. And the toadlets must have an even worse problem in mid-summer; no one seems to have thought much about them. Scientific studies have indicated that toad road deaths are unlikely to pose a serious threat to a population, though they look, and indeed are, horrific spectacles. Whether or not there is a sound conservation case for helping toad jaywalkers, there clearly is a compassionate one. County naturalists trusts, the British Herpetological Society and others carry out these rescues, which are also excellent ways of encouraging communities to become involved with their local toad ponds — the soundest possible base for conservation.

The breeding season

When frogs and toads get to their ponds the business of breeding really begins. At least, sometimes it does. For many frogs, arriving at odd times in February, there is quite a long wait and all they seem to do is sit around on the pond bottom. This has been called the 'pre-spawning period', and it can last several weeks as numbers gradually build up. Any females arriving are quickly grabbed by males, in the

Frogs in amplexus.

'amplexus' embrace just behind the front legs. The males then become passengers, and have to go wherever the female decides to swim. Females which arrive early, or hibernate in the breeding pond, run a serious risk of being grabbed by one or more males as early as January and then held in tight embrace for weeks or even months on end. Such prolonged amplexus often results in wounding, or even death by drowning of the unfortunate female on the receiving end of such ardour. Sooner or later, something – we're not sure what – 'triggers' the frogs, and spawning begins. After dark, they all move up into shallow water (just a few centimetres deep, if possible), usually all together in one particular part of the pond. The males now make their subdued, 'purring' croaks; this is the noisiest time of year for amphibians, but it has to be said that the common frog is not an impressive performer compared with many other species. Even a large colony often cannot be heard more than a few dozen yards away. What they lack in voice they do, however, make up for in determination and there's a lot of fighting, with rival males trying to force off ones already paired up with females. This doesn't seem to succeed very often, and the male's grip is so tight that the female's chest may be injured by it. Once spawning has started the frogs may be active in daytime as well as at night, and with care it is possible to creep up on a colony and watch what is going on. The water is alive with splashes and kicks, frogs scampering about everywhere, with a background of the feeble croaking going on all the time. The males have very thick forelimbs and extra-flabby skins at this time of year, and their throats have a distinctly bluish tinge. Females, on the other hand, are almost obscenely fat with their loads of spawn. Egg-laying is mainly done in the depths of the night, usually around 3 a.m. according to those with the patience to stay up and watch. It's all very sudden; the female helps by pressing her hands on her belly, and the spawn is ejected as a single mass within a matter of seconds. Fertilization is external and the male has to be quick off the mark, shedding his sperms precisely as the eggs are laid. The spawn 'jelly' quickly swells in the water, and after only a few minutes the eggs are no longer accessible to sperms, and will not therefore be fertilized. The male releases the now very skinny-looking female, who promptly swims away from the breeding colony to hide in a quieter part of the pond. For her it is all over, but the male will seek another mate if he can find one. Most of the females lay within a few days of each other, and close together so that a large 'mat', made up of many individual spawn clumps stuck together, gets formed. After a week or so activity falls off, with the frogs drifting away to other parts of the pond or leaving the water altogether. They don't eat anything while they are breeding, and, coming so soon after the fast of hibernation, many frogs are left too weak to survive. The bodies of these exhausted individuals are a common and grisly sight around the breeding ponds.

If frog breeding sounds a frenzied affair, that of common toads is even more so.

No pre-spawning period here, but a mass 'splash down' into the pond, a rapid burst of spawning (which goes on day and night without interruption unless the weather turns cold) and then away. Toads prefer deeper water than frogs (say 9 inches to a foot, 20–30 cm or so), and, although they have the same kind of amplexus embrace, the eggs are laid as long strings rather than squat clumps. This means that their behaviour has to be a bit different too, because a string of eggs can't be shot out all at one go. What happens is that the male 'feels' with his toes when the eggs start to emerge, and sheds his sperm over them until the female stops for a rest. The whole business takes several hours, with bursts of spawning interrupted by 15-minute breaks. During this time the pair is anchored by the spawn string, which is usually wound around water plants and ends up some 2–3 yards (metres) long. Presumably eggs spread out in a string will be better oxygenated than those in a mass like frog spawn, but we really don't know why the two species have evolved such different spawning procedures.

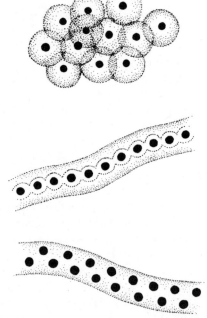

Spawn of frog (top), *natterjack* (centre) *and common toad* (bottom).

The actual business of egg-laying in natterjacks is similar to that of common toads, but other aspects of breeding are very different. For one thing, natterjacks are our noisiest amphibian and choruses of males set up an incredible racket with their 'rrrrup'-type croaks. The noise is made by pumping air backwards and forwards between the lungs and the vocal sac, all sealed in by the nostril valves (see p. 41). In the natterjack this vocal sac is a large swelling under the chin which, when fully expanded, makes the head look 2–3 times its normal size – a quite unforgettable sight. Even a small colony of natterjacks can be heard about a mile (1–2 km) away if the wind is in the right direction. The season goes on much longer for this species than for common frogs and toads, usually for about 2 months, from mid-April to mid-June. Females are likely to turn up at any time during this period, though there are usually a few spawning 'peaks' on warm, wet nights. Some females may even lay twice in the same year. The spawn is laid in very shallow water, normally less than 6 inches (15 cm) deep, and has just one row of eggs. This distinguishes it from common toad spawn, which has a double row. Natterjack males don't fight very much, but seem to rely mainly on the loudness of their croaks to intimidate smaller males and thus win themselves more mates. They're less

Male natterjack calling.

frantic about the whole business of breeding, and unlike the common species are quite happy to feed except when actually in amplexus. Individual males may hang around the ponds for the full length of the breeding season (though they usually hide up by day, and only come out at night), whereas females just visit the water for a few hours to spawn and then leave immediately. If you visit a natterjack colony you will usually see lots of males but very few females.

Toads in rivers

Frogs and toads can still surprise us, with new aspects of their biology being discovered all the time. A minor but interesting recent example relates to spawning in running water, rather than the normal stagnant ponds. There are occasional accounts of frogs spawning in streams, even quite fast-flowing ones, and gluing their eggs to some suitable support. Heaven knows what happens to any tadpoles hatching under these kinds of conditions. More recently, toads have been noticed spawning in deep rivers. It's one of those situations where someone casually mentions seeing toad tadpoles in a river, someone else pipes up with 'funny you should say that . . .' and so on. It may even turn out to be quite common. A few years ago I came across it myself, with large numbers of toad taddies apparently thriving in still water just behind a weir in a French salmon river. It would be interesting to know how successful these breeding sites are, and how toads choose them.

Deep croak

Breeding activities of frogs and toads have recently become popular subjects among scientists investigating animal behaviour. Studies on the croaking of toads, and the ways in which males compete for females, have been particularly fascinating. It turns out that the pitch of a toad's croak is related to its body size; the larger the male (females are mute), the deeper the croak. When a male common toad latches onto a female, he is likely to be attacked by other males trying to usurp his position; if this happens, the resident male makes a croak. The attacker can then judge, from the pitch of this croak, whether to continue with the assault. If the incumbent sounds 'small', it may well be worthwhile; if, on the other hand, he sounds 'big', it might be wise to get off. People used to assume that the female had no say in any of this and just got lumbered with whatever male happened to grab her first; but it turns out that she can be quite sneaky. If a male jumps on that the female decides isn't big enough to fertilize her eggs properly, she can move into a part of the pond with lots of spare males hanging around and so cause a fight. As we've seen, this will often result in her getting what she wanted — a bigger male on her back — but there is a serious risk involved too. Successful displacement of a male occasionally triggers a mass attack by all the males in the vicinity, resulting in a struggling 'ball' of toads in which the female is often drowned.

Natterjacks, with their much louder croaks, have a different and more civilized approach. Instead of making a mad scramble for females, the males space themselves out around the pond and call to attract females to them. Females will go to any croaker, but pitch is again important, because a smaller, high-pitched male is likely to have his territory taken over by a bigger one. This is altogether a more gentlemanly affair than the goings-on of common toads, and is usually settled without a fight. Generally speaking a small male gives in gracefully to a larger competitor, but some are really crafty and lurk silently nearby trying to intercept females en route to their noisy companion. So a toad pond isn't the random cacophony of sound it at first seems, but a den of intrigue and competition for the only success that really matters — fathering some tadpoles of the next generation.

Hybrids and other freaks

It's not uncommon in some places to see 'mixed' pairs of frogs and toads, especially male frogs on the backs of female toads. Since spawning is so different in these species, you wouldn't expect even the first step of such a union – fertilization – to be successful, and it isn't. Common toad and natterjack pairs also crop up though, and in this case fertilization sometimes works. Development is poor, and it's rare indeed for the spawn even to get as far as hatching. Very careful treatment in the laboratory has resulted in just one or two hybrid toadlets, which look mainly like common toads with no yellow stripe but a few minor natterjack features such as green irises in their eyes. Their 'vigour' is so low that it's extremely unlikely they ever survive in the wild.

Generally speaking mixed pairs amount to a waste of effort by both partners, and evolution has tended to minimize their occurrence with behavioural barriers, different breeding season times and so on. However, it's only fair to add that in some cases hybridization not only works but has important biological consequences. The so-called 'green frogs' are a good example; sorting out the relationships of the 3 major European species (pool, edible and marsh frogs, all of which have been successfully introduced into Britain – see p. 105 – and all of which look very similar) has been a mindboggling exercise in genetics. It turns out that the edible frog is in fact a stable, fertile hybrid of marsh and pool frogs; furthermore, there are at least 4 'strains' of edible frogs which can only be told apart by breeding experiments – to the observer they look identical. Quite possibly this kind of situation is evolution in action, and the beginnings of a totally new species.

Apart from hybrids, other freaks crop up from time to time. Albino frogs and, much more rarely, toads have been reported and I have seen frogs with extra front

or back legs. These grow because amphibians have good powers of tissue regeneration, and an injury in the right place can lead to the production of an entire extra limb. I've also seen a male frog with a single front leg, which must be a disaster at breeding time when he is supposed to be grabbing females. But in the tough world of natural selection, no animal with a serious disability will last for long; you have to look at an awful lot of frogs or toads to have a good chance of finding anything unusual, simply because the lives of such specimens are likely to be even shorter than those of their normal brethren.

Tadpole life

Once the eggs are laid, the parents have nothing more to do with them. They're on their own, and precious few are going to make it. Ever wondered why frog eggs are so big? They're about 100 times the diameter of a human egg (not including the jelly, which isn't really part of the egg itself), and, as any mathematician will tell you, that means they are some one million times the internal volume. The reason is really quite straightforward; unlike human or other mammalian babes, they will get no more food from their parents, yet it will be some time before they can swim and feed themselves. To tide them over until hatching, the eggs are packed with all the goodies needed for the early stages of development. One of these is a dark pigment, called melanin, which helps the eggs to absorb warmth from the spring sunshine and grow into tadpoles as quickly as possible. Hatching time is very variable, depending almost entirely on the weather. Frog eggs laid in a cold spring may take three weeks, whereas natterjack spawn in early summer can hatch in just a few days. This is actually one of the safest times in a frog's life, because very few animals eat frog or toad spawn. Moorhens sometimes have a go at it, and so do newts, flatworms and small boys, but it doesn't seem to have a very wide appeal. A more serious risk is fungus infection. In particularly cold springs you may find frog or toad spawn entirely destroyed by white, threadlike fungi growing all over it like cotton wool. Actual freezing of spawn also happens sometimes, and this too is usually fatal.

The eggs gradually grow and become oblong, and finally break free of the rotting jelly all around them. They are now tadpoles, and this is where their troubles really begin. For the lucky few, normal growth and development over the following weeks involves a general increase in size, the appearance of the hindleg 'buds' at the base of the tail, and finally the change into a fully-fledged froglet or toadlet, a process known as 'metamorphosis'. The period of tadpole life for common frogs and toads, from egg to metamorphosis, usually occupies something like 12 weeks. Natterjacks are much quicker, getting the whole thing over with in 6–8 weeks – even as few as 4 under very favourable conditions. Virtually all of tadpole life is spent swimming around looking for something to eat, usually among water plants or on the silty pond bottom. Algae and single-celled animals (protozoa) are the main foods, but particular delicacies are dead animals or bits of meat. Adult frogs which died of exhaustion after spawning, or sick fellow tadpoles are greedily relished by this cannibalistic brotherhood. Frog taddies start off sociable, sticking together as a writhing black mass when they first hatch. They soon change their ways though, and larger ones become very secretive, hiding up in mud or water plants for much of the day. Toad tadpoles are more extrovert, and even large

Frog tadpole

Toad tadpole

ones spend a lot of time swimming in open water. Telling frog and toad tadpoles apart is quite easy; frog ones are brownish with a gold speckling, whereas toad taddies are jet black. But it's much more difficult to distinguish natterjack tadpoles from common toad ones, and even experts have trouble doing this. The only safe things to say are that very small (less than 15 mm long) black tadpoles in sand dune ponds in May or June are very likely to be natterjack; so are any larger black taddies with a white patch under their 'chins', but a lot of natterjack tadpoles don't get this patch until near metamorphosis, so its absence doesn't mean much.

Tadpoles seem to make a scrumptious meal for almost every carnivore in or around the ponds, and for the vast majority of taddies their first few days of life will be their last. The list of predators is staggering: water beetles of dozens of species

Great diving beetle catching tadpole prey.

and their larvae, dragonfly nymphs, water boatmen and water scorpions will eat all kinds of tadpoles. These creatures kill their prey with piercing and sucking mouthparts, sucking out the contents and leaving the skin as a shrivelled mess. Toad poisons, though present in the skins of their tadpoles from an early age, are no defence against them. Other marauders such as newts, fish, water shrews and birds like ducks and thrushes will often leave toad taddies alone. They swallow their prey whole, and prefer to stick to the tastier frog tadpoles which they consume in enormous numbers. Experiments have been done to see just how many tadpoles some of these creatures will eat. Great diving beetles cause appalling carnage, easily managing 20 large tadpoles a day, and it has been calculated that a single pair of great crested newts can account for all the tadpoles produced by a pair of frogs during the course of a spring.

To make matters worse, there's also competition between tadpoles of different species. Frog taddies, for example, secrete some kind of growth inhibitor which, if things get too crowded, can really screw up smaller common toad or natterjack tadpoles in the same pond. And on top of all that, there are catastrophic accidents. A herd of cows coming down for a drink or a bathe on a warm afternoon may trample the daylights out of an entire tadpole population (or drink them), and lots of taddies die just by getting trapped in small puddles which dry up as the water level drops in early summer. In the light of all this, perhaps the most surprising thing is that any tadpoles manage to survive at all. Being born a tadpole must make for one of the worst life insurance risks imaginable.

Peter Pan syndrome

As with human beings, a small minority of tadpoles are reluctant to grow up. This Peter Pan syndrome is called 'neoteny', and results in the tadpole growing larger and larger but never turning into a froglet. It's commoner in newts than in frogs or toads, but is quite often seen in the edible frog, Rana esculenta. The exact reason isn't known, but cold ponds seem particularly prone to having neotenous tadpoles. They can live for a year or more, and grow as long as 5 inches (120 mm). Neoteny can be induced artificially by keeping frog or toad tadpoles at low temperatures, and after a while the condition cannot be reversed by warming them up again, so cold conditions in the wild probably are an important natural cause.

Metamorphosis and juvenile life: growing up

It's a common belief that a tadpole just gradually turns into a frog, but the reality is not quite like that. For most of its life, a tadpole is simply growing larger. Admittedly some subtle but important changes do go on during this period of growth, but the major transformation into a four-legged hopper is actually quite abrupt. When it has reached the necessary size, hormones start to flow and the change over from water to land happens in a few days. A pond brimming with tadpoles one day may be almost deserted a week later. Metamorphosis is obviously a very complicated biological process, and there is still a lot to be learnt about it. The most dramatic changes include the absorption of the tail (it's not shed, as was once thought, but economically reabsorbed), the appearance of the legs, the switch to lung breathing and a new texture and colour to the skin. Needless to say there are many internal changes too. The events of metamorphosis span the time of transition from water to land-living. Front legs appear while the tadpole is still in the pond, but final disappearance of the tail is delayed until the frog- or toadlet is out on dry land.

Leaving the water is yet another dangerous time. Apart from the serious risk of being trodden on by something, or somebody, birds such as thrushes and blackbirds have caught on to the benefits of this ready supply of food and often make a fair killing round the pond edges. Curiously, after metamorphosis froglets and toadlets drown very easily if they can't climb out of the water, and often do. Small boys with collecting jars please note – if you must catch baby frogs or toads, handle them very gently and make sure that they are not carried around in a jar of water; damp moss or grass is much better, but really they should be left alone at this stage of life. Another hazard is the sun. Baby natterjacks especially suffer from frizzling up on the sand around the pond as they try to head for cover, and many die crossing these mini-deserts every year. It's so serious that they have evolved a way of trying to cope with this particular problem, by clustering together in little 'mounds' of toadlets in an attempt to conserve moisture.

Midsummer is the time for metamorphosis, and the froglets and toadlets hang around the edge of the pond under whatever cover they can find until conditions arise which allow them to disperse. This usually means a thunderstorm or some such downpour, soaking the warm ground all around. Then, for a day or two, the countryside seems to come alive with tiny frogs and toads scampering away into the wide open spaces. No doubt this kind of thing has given rise to some of the old stories about raining frogs and plagues of frogs, perhaps including the famous Old

DEVELOPMENT AND METAMORPHOSIS OF THE
COMMON FROG: *Rana temporaria*

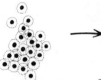

3. Development begins within 2–3 hours of fertilization. The embryo lengthens, becoming ovoid in shape after 3–7 days, soon followed by further growth and differentiation into a more obvious tadpole.

1. As the female expels them, the eggs are fertilized by the male frog and sink to the bottom of the water.

2. The outer jelly layer quickly swells with water and the eggs float to the surface where they adhere together forming the mass known as 'spawn'.

4. After about 2 weeks the wriggling tadpole frees itself but remains attached to the jelly by means of sticky suckers behind the mouth while more development occurs.

5. Rasping 'teeth' form for feeding on filamentous algae and the tadpole breathes via external gills on each side of the body.

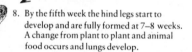

7. The operculum fuses completely with the body except on the left side where an opening called the spiracle remains. This facilitates the ejection of water from the internal gills.

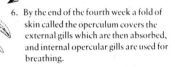

6. By the end of the fourth week a fold of skin called the operculum covers the external gills which are then absorbed, and internal opercular gills are used for breathing.

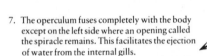

8. By the fifth week the hind legs start to develop and are fully formed at 7–8 weeks. A change from plant to plant and animal food occurs and lungs develop.

9. The tadpole stops feeding by the twelfth week. The outer skin is cast, the mouth widens, the tongue grows, and eyelids form. The right forelimb grows through the operculum and the left through the spiracle.

12. Fully formed, the young frog leaves the water but stays in a damp environment where it eats tiny insects, gaining as much weight as possible before the winter hibernation.

10. The intestines shorten and the abdomen becomes flatter. The tail which weighs as much as one third of the total body weight is gradually resorbed, providing much needed nutrition while this metamorphosis occurs.

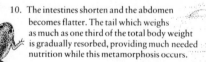

11. Now looking more like a small frog, it can swim with its hind legs and crawl out onto land. The rest of the tail is resorbed.

Testament version. But it doesn't last long. Predators have another beanfeast, and the survivors settle down to a slightly safer life on land.

Surprisingly little is known about what happens between this point in a frog's life and the time it becomes mature two or three years later. Obviously it's a period of rapid growth; baby natterjacks leaving their ponds a pitiful 7 or 8 mm long in June may be 4 times bigger by the time they start hibernating in October. Apart from that, they are generally assumed to live more or less like adults except that they don't migrate to breeding ponds in the spring. A few differences are known: baby natterjacks in their first summer are active on bright sunny days and don't come out at all at night – quite the opposite of their parents. By their first autumn they are adopting 'adult' ways, and can just about cope with digging their own burrows in the sand. This growing up phase is also the time of great dispersal, where new ground may be broken and new ponds eventually colonized. One hill I know in Surrey provides a fascinating example of just how adventurous these little beasts are. It's well over 50 yards (metres) high, and right on top is a sunken pit which effectively traps any animal that falls into it. There is no water on the hill, and the nearest pond is some way away, but every year the pit traps a good crop of toadlets in the weeks after midsummer. I can't imagine there is anything on this hill which attracts the baby toads, they are just a small sample of the great outpouring going on all around at this time of year.

How long does it take a frog to grow to breeding age? Well, for common frogs two full years seem to be enough for both sexes. An egg laid in spring 1984, for example, will, in the unlikely event of it surviving, return as an adult to lay its own eggs in the spring of 1986. Male toads can also mature in two years, but females seem to take a year longer. This is true of both common toads and natterjacks, and was nicely proved at a site where natterjack spawn was introduced for the first time a few years ago. Males appeared and started croaking two years later, but no spawn was laid. Females came down to the pond the following year. There is a lot of variation between individuals, and between populations too. Some slower-growing males can take three years to mature, and slow female toads four years or even longer. Compare all this with mice, which can breed a few weeks after they are born. Baby frogs and toads can be 'sexed' by dissection within a few weeks of metamorphosis, but unfortunately it's not possible to tell male from female juveniles just by looking.

How many frogs are there?

There are several ways of answering this seemingly simple question; it all depends exactly what you mean. For instance, nobody has tried to count baby frogs, let alone tadpoles, so estimates only really apply to adults, although there may be as many immature animals as mature ones. About 50 years ago Maxwell Savage 'guesstimated' that there were somewhere between 3–6 frogs per acre (6–12 frogs per hectare) where he lived – say 5 on average – just north of London. If you multiply that up to the size of Britain, you arrive at a total population around the 300 million mark – about 10 frogs for every person back in the 1930s. Much later, Arnold Cooke carried out a more systematic survey and by the 1970s it looked as if the frog population was down to about one fiftieth of its prewar levels – say 6–8 million frogs, or 1 frog per 8 people at that time. Of course none of these figures can be taken very seriously. We've already seen how different habitats can support different numbers of frogs, and the error limits on these enormous numbers may be of the same scale as the numbers themselves. But they do show that, at least in the recent past, frogs were very common animals. Toads are probably less numerous, but still to be rated in millions. With natterjacks we can be a bit more precise, because they only live now in about 30 places in Britain and their populations can be counted individually. There are thought to be 20,000–30,000 natterjacks in Britain, which sounds a lot until you compare it with the estimates for the other two species.

More serious work on population sizes has been done by looking at small areas of the country. With frogs, one thing you can do is count the number of spawn clumps in ponds each spring. Since females only lay a single clump each, this will straightaway give an estimate of the numbers of females. You can do the same thing with natterjacks, this time counting their spawn strings, which are usually laid separately and in pretty conspicuous places. Common toads are more difficult, because they tend to mix up their spawn together, making it impossible to count. Another way is to use a so-called 'mark-recapture' method. What you do is catch a few animals, mark them so you can recognize them again (with a waterproof waistband, for instance) and then let them go. A day or so later you catch another lot in the same area, and see how many are carrying your mark. In its simplest form, you can then make a direct calculation as to how many animals there are in the area. The logic goes like this: if, say, you caught and marked 10 frogs originally, and then caught another 5 the next night including 2 with your 'waistband' on, your estimate of the total number of frogs = $10 \div 2 \times 5 = 25$. This is because your second catch shows that for every 2 frogs marked there were still 3 unmarked; since you originally marked 10, there must altogether be 15 unmarked ones around somewhere. To do it properly the maths are a bit more complicated than this, but the principle isn't difficult to understand. There are problems with all of these methods, unfortunately. For instance, counting spawn may tell you how many females there are, but what about the males? It isn't safe to assume that there are equal numbers of both sexes, and at toad breeding sites males often outnumber females by 3 to 1 or even more. Perhaps the best method has been developed by Paul Gittins in Wales; this involves completely surrounding a pond with a 'frog-proof' fence, and setting traps at intervals all the way round it. Animals trying to get in are stopped by the fence and blunder into the traps, from which they are lifted out, counted, and put on the pond side of the fence. This kind of study needs, among other things, a vandal-proof site and a lot of hard work, but it does provide an excellent way of estimating frog, toad and newt populations.

It looks as if most ponds support somewhere between 10 to 200–300 frogs; higher numbers are exceptional, but they do occur and were probably a lot commoner in the past. A colony of 1,000 frogs today is an exceptionally large one, but as a boy I can remember ponds which must at the very least have been visited by several hundred frogs each year. Even now in some garden ponds (including my own) you can sometimes find colonies of 100–200 animals in really quite tiny bits of water; it shows what they can do if conditions are right, sadly a much rarer situation in the countryside than it used to be.

The size of toad colonies also varies a lot; many are quite small, but some are larger than the biggest frog ones. Partly this is because they are fussier about their breeding sites, and all the toads in an area will often congregate in just a few ponds rather than spreading themselves more thinly as frogs do. Colonies of many thousands of toads are not uncommon even today where the habitat is suitable. Paul Gittins's study lake in Wales regularly attracts about 6,000 toads every spring, and at the other extreme I know of garden ponds that get just a few pairs. Natterjack populations are very variable too, with much the same sort of range as seen with common toads.

So we return to the question of how many frogs and toads a given area of land can support. Savage suggested 3–6 per acre (7–15 per hectare), and this still seems quite a reasonable sort of figure for some habitats. Of course it can be less; I doubt if there's one frog per thousand acres in the most intensively farmed arable areas. And it can be more; on one summer evening I counted 34 adult frogs foraging in my back garden, a density of about 200 frogs per acre (600 frogs per hectare)!

Newts

Britain's 3 species of anurans represent just half of this country's tiny amphibian fauna. The other half is made up by 3 species of newts, the so-called 'urodeles' or tailed amphibians. Most schoolchildren have probably caught newts at some time or other; basically they look like lizards, but aren't scaly and move much more slowly. They also spend a lot of time in the water, where they are good swimmers and look much more at home than they do on land. Our three natives are the smooth or common newt, *Triturus vulgaris*; the palmate newt, *Triturus helveticus*; and the great crested or warty newt, *Triturus cristatus*. As their name suggests, common newts are the most abundant in many parts of the country and can be found in spring in all sorts of ponds and ditches, especially in lowland areas. This is also the only kind of newt native to Ireland. Adults usually grow 3–4 inches (75–100 mm) long, and males have a high, wavy crest on their back and tail during the breeding season. Both sexes have yellow/orange bellies, normally with a good number of black spots – altogether very attractive creatures. Palmate newts are a bit smaller (about 3 inches, 75 mm) and are quite often found in the same ponds as common newts. They're very rare in the east Midlands and East Anglia, but

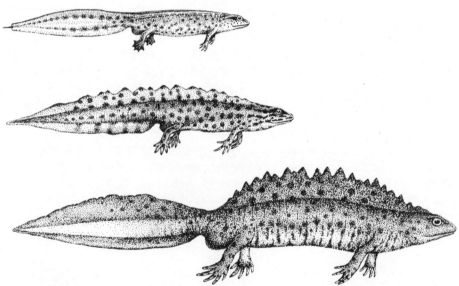

The three species of British newts: male palmate newt (top), *common newt* (centre) *and great crested newt* (bottom).

frequently more common than 'common' newts in heathy or mountainous places. Males don't have much of a crest, but their tails look chopped off at the end, with a thin black filament trailing out behind for a few mm. They have webbed hindfeet, another distinctive feature. Female palmates, though, don't have any of these things and can be difficult to tell apart from female common newts. The best guide is the colour of their bellies and throats, which in palmates tend to be paler (throats are often pink) without spots, but even experts sometimes have trouble so it's usually best to rely on males for identification.

There's no mistaking the great crested newt. It's much bigger than the other two species (6 inches, 150 mm or so) and more heavily built. The adult is dark in colour, and from above looks almost black when in the water. Underneath both sexes are beautifully marked with yellow-orange and black blotches. Males, as their name suggests, have high, jagged crests on their backs and a silver stripe along their tails. It's difficult to imagine more impressive animals, and they have always been much prized by children wielding pond nets. They live in much the same places as common newts, but are generally far less abundant and were protected, like the natterjack, by the Wildlife and Countryside Act of 1981. Catching or keeping these newts in captivity, or hurting them in any way, is now illegal other than under licence.

The basic biology of all three species is much the same. Mostly they hibernate under suitable cover on land (see p. 57), although individuals of all three species can sometimes be found overwintering in ponds. Early in spring they all head for water, and when they arrive spend much longer there than frogs or toads do. It's quite usual for newts to migrate to ponds during February and March, and stay until May or June. They're there to reproduce, but courtship is a much more gentlemanly affair than the 'grab what you can' approach of frogs and toads. Males do not embrace females at all, but chase them around and perform elaborate displays instead. It's easy, and quite fascinating, to watch this in any well stocked garden pond. The males dash in front, arch their backs, and vibrate their tails very fast to send their smell towards a receptive female. If all goes well, a small bag of sperms is dropped on the floor of the pond and the female moves over to pick it up with her cloaca. Fertilization is internal – another difference from frogs and toads. Newts also produce far fewer eggs, just a few hundred usually, and the females lay them one at a time. They're very careful about this, wrapping each egg individually in the leaf of a water plant. Newt tadpoles don't look at all like frog or toad ones; in fact they are miniature versions of their parents, but with big feathery gills sticking out where you would expect ears to be. They grow up through the summer and usually metamorphose in August or September, although some stay in the pond until the following spring. Newt taddies take a bit of finding, but poking around in pondweed in July will usually come up with a few. Crested newt tadpoles grow as

Fish are major predators of newt tadpoles.

big as adult palmates and are easy to identify, but common and palmate taddies are small, brown and almost impossible to tell apart.

Adult newts and their tadpoles are entirely carnivorous. In the ponds they will eat anything they can catch, from water shrimps and small worms to frog tadpoles. Sometimes two newts grab opposite ends of the same worm, and a vigorous fight follows until the weaker one is shaken off (or the worm breaks). The adults leave the pond by midsummer and spend their days hiding in long grass or under stones and logs. On damp nights they come out to hunt worms, small slugs and other beasties – more good friends for the gardener. Newts have much the same enemies as frogs and toads. Crested newts have warty skins (hence their alternative name), which produce poisons like toads do, so they probably suffer less predation than the smaller species. Fish, even sticklebacks, are major enemies of newt taddies and should be kept out of any garden pond if you want a good population of newts to develop.

Newts take 2 or 3 years to reach maturity, and in captivity have lived for more than 20. No doubt few, if any, survive that long in the wild. Losses of ponds in the countryside have affected newts badly, especially the great crested, which tends to prefer the deeper ones, and it's just as important to conserve them as it is to try and help frogs and toads. A really good newt pond can have all 3 species living side by side, but sites like this are rare and precious finds these days.

Herpetology and the law

Like almost everything else in our lives, the way we treat frogs and toads is sometimes the concern of lawyers. There are many Acts of Parliament which have some bearing on the subject; for instance, it's just as illegal to be cruel to a frog or toad as it is to a rabbit or a cow. One piece of legislation, however, deals with these animals in a more specific way: the Wildlife and Countryside Act of 1981. This holds the all-time record for the number of amendments it was subjected to on the way to becoming law; despite that, many people feel it to be one of the least effective Acts ever enabled, in terms of what it set out to do – ensure the conservation of our countryside and its wildlife. But that's another story.

Under the 1981 Act, it is forbidden to *sell* common frogs or toads, or their spawn or tadpoles, without a licence from the Department of the Environment. It is *not* illegal for individuals like you and me to go and catch a few for our own private purposes. The reasons behind these rules are a bit difficult to fathom, at least they are for me. For very many decades enormous numbers of frogs – hundreds of thousands probably – have been collected every year in Britain and Ireland, by commercial dealers, mainly for sale to schools and research institutes. It was shown some while back that the areas from which these frogs are collected are among the few which have *not* suffered serious declines in their frog populations; this is not as odd as it sounds, because collectors will only bother to keep going to places with lots of frogs when they need to supply that large a market. They have stayed in business because in healthy environments frogs can easily stand this amount of cropping. The real problems have arisen when the habitats have been altered or destroyed, with catastrophic consequences for frogs and toads (among many other things); yet the Act has virtually no teeth in this crucial area. A final irony is that the licensing procedure is only a formality anyway, and anyone applying to sell frogs or toads is more or less automatically given permission.

The natterjack is, at least theoretically, better protected under the 1981 Act than the two common species. Not only does commercial sale require a licence, but so does *anyone* who wants to touch, take or otherwise molest these toads (or their spawn or tadpoles). Furthermore these licences (this time from the Nature Conservancy Council) are not so readily given. Even so, the same criticisms still apply. Human 'predation' is of negligible significance to natterjacks in comparison with habitat losses, and the police have enough to do without trying to sort out whether the toad in young Jimmy's hand is a common one (OK, sonny) or a natterjack (accompany-me-to-the-station).

Another part of the 1981 Act makes it illegal to import almost any species of frog to Britain. Technically you can apply to the DoE for an import licence, but in

practice this won't be given without an export licence from the country of origin, which in turn is usually impossible to obtain. This applies not just to commercial dealers, but to anyone popping across to France for a holiday and hoping to sneak back with a few edible frogs for their garden pond, or some such thing. The penalty for letting an 'alien' species go in Britain is an *unlimited* fine, potentially much more severe than the punishments for most other kinds of petty crime.

The value of these kinds of law is of course very much a matter of opinion. Mine, for what it's worth, is that they're not a great deal of use. Such laws can't really help to conserve species since this can only be done effectively by protecting and managing their habitats – something no government has yet been prepared to have a proper go at. Of course the 1981 Act might just stop someone taking the last few natterjacks from a tiny colony, or bring the culprits to heel if they were caught trying it. And it does draw public attention to wildlife conservation problems, which has some merit in itself. On the other hand, it conjures up a 'big brother' image of trying to stop people, especially children, learning first-hand about wild creatures by catching one or two and keeping them for a while. This is the way I got to be interested in frogs and toads, and it would alarm me to think that future generations could be prevented by law from doing this kind of thing. To put it crudely, children prevented from catching tadpoles today mean even fewer people interested enough to care about them tomorrow.

Conservation

We live in an age of rapid changes in the countryside, quite different from the slow pace of rural life that our forefathers knew. One result of this has been the devastation of much of the wildlife we used to take for granted, including a good number of frogs and toads. These creatures have disappeared, or become rare, over vast tracts of lowland England where up to the last war they abounded. In most cases the reasons are fairly clear: ponds have been drained or allowed to silt up by neglect – very few farmers need them any more, preferring to water their livestock with troughs – and arable 'desertification' has spread like wildfire from the Fens and other East Anglian lowlands to the Sussex Downs. Not only does this cause ponds to be filled in or ploughed up, but those remaining often become horribly polluted with silage, fertilizers and all the other 'agrochemicals' so widely used by farmers today. Fifty years ago the Downs had about three ponds per square mile of land; now more than 70% have gone, and their wildlife – including frogs and toads – with them. True, West Country, Welsh and Scottish upland areas haven't yet suffered as badly (although recent grant-aid schemes for the reclamation of marginal land, and the traumas of acid rain pose threats even here), and garden ponds have provided a very successful new habitat; but nevertheless, most of England is still covered by farms and in these very large areas there can be no

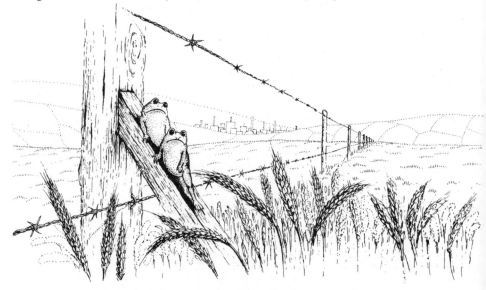

Male: *I know the family pond is here somewhere.*
Female: *Perhaps we should give up now and try again next year?*

doubting the declines that have gone on. Natterjacks have been unfortunate enough to choose two particularly vulnerable habitats: the lowland sandy heaths of southern England and East Anglia have been decimated by forestry plantations, self-sown pines, excessive fires and a host of other assaults, with the result that natterjacks have been almost exterminated on heathland. Sand dunes have been prime targets for holidaymakers and the holiday industry. Before the last war, for example, natterjacks lived on dunes along the coast of North Wales. Since then, almost every square yard has had a caravan or holiday chalet put on top of it and natterjacks are now totally extinct in Wales. Overall, this species is thought to have suffered a decline of 75–80% during the present century.

So there's plenty to be concerned about. The question is: what can be done to remedy the situation? Certainly there's no need to take a defeatist view, and it's surprising what a bit of enthusiasm can achieve. At the simplest level, anyone with a garden can make a pond in it. In the part of Sussex where I live, the results from doing this have been particularly dramatic. Rural areas have almost no frogs or toads – just the odd, tiny colony here and there for mile after mile. But in the town it's a different story. In a district with about 125,000 households a survey I carried out a few years ago indicated the existence of more than 7,000 ponds used by frogs, and around 2,000 toad breeding sites – an astonishing backyard success story. Just in the 150 or so houses closest to my own home there are some 22 ponds, virtually all of which are used by frogs or toads.

Another thing to do is to take up the cudgels for any local ponds you happen to know about; or if you don't know of any, why not start a survey and see what you can find? This has been done on quite a large scale in places as far apart as Brighton and Durham; it involves contacting the landowners, and organizing local volunteers (there's always a County Naturalists' Trust Conservation Corps, or local branch of the British Trust for Conservation Volunteers somewhere near you) to do any work necessary to restore a good pool to its former glory. It's a good idea to contact one of these organizations, and the British Herpetological Society (see p. 118), if you're interested in this kind of thing and cash in on their hard-won experience and expertise. The sort of work that gets done includes trimming away too many overhanging bushes to let the light in, shovelling out silt, and fencing off from access by too many cattle. It's hard work, but very satisfying, to end up with a pond packed with animals and plants where once there was a dingy puddle. Of course there are some politics involved; a tactful approach to landowners is one of the first things you learn in this game, but this too has its pleasures. An angling club in Surrey recently gave up its rights to stock a pond with fish when told of its importance to amphibians, a marvellous gesture and demonstration of the goodwill that can be achieved when things go right.

Natterjack toad conservation is a more specialized business, but there are people doing it and some good successes have been scored. Work on heathland involves cutting down encroaching trees and scrub (the opposite of what many people think conservation is about) to maintain the open habitat, as a replacement for the grazing animals that once did the same job rather more effectively. New ponds have also been specially designed and built for natterjacks, and recently the toad was successfully reintroduced to one of its old haunts by the Royal Society for the Protection of Birds and the British Herpetological Society working together.

Above all this are the serious politics of conservation: lobbying for changes in the law to alter the balance in favour of wildlife, and fighting local issues as they crop up. Many of the 'voluntary' organizations, such as the British Herpetological Society, Friends of the Earth, Royal Society for the Protection of Birds, Fauna and Flora Preservation Society, County Naturalists Trusts and others co-operate in this through a body known as 'Wildlife Link'. And of course there is the statutory government organization, the Nature Conservancy Council. But even put together they don't have a great deal of political 'clout' as yet – you can see that from the state things are in – although circumstances may be slowly changing. Combined membership of the voluntary conservation movement now runs into hundreds of thousands of people, and recent opinion polls have shown that a clear majority of the population is concerned to see proper and effective conservation of our national wildlife heritage. It is also increasingly being realized that many of the worst excesses of arable farming and pinewood forestry amount to a kind of economic madness, with subsidies causing overproduction and wastage on a scandalous scale. Hopefully this realization (particularly by the taxpayers who fund it all) may soon begin to count more strongly in favour of conservation.

I became a conservationist when 'the' pond I knew as a child was filled in and a housing estate put on top of it. A thriving community of frogs, toads, newts, dragonflies, water plants and so many other things, as well as a very beautiful place, was annihilated in a matter of days. Of course this pond had no national significance, there weren't any very rare species or suchlike, but that wasn't the point. It showed in miniature what was going on all over the country; the threat was very real, and it still is.

Frogs in gardens

Whenever there is talk of frogs and toads declining and being in need of conservation, someone often pipes up with, 'Well, I've got plenty in my garden,' or words to that effect. And it's perfectly true; it is in the artificial habitat of gardens that these animals have continued to do well despite all the problems out in the 'natural' countryside. Gardens are now such an important habitat for frogs and toads that it's worth giving them some special thought, and what I will do here is to try and answer some of the questions most often raised by people interested in having frogs in their gardens.

Q: Should I encourage frogs and toads in my garden? What use are they?

A: Yes you should, for two main reasons. Firstly, they have declined very much in the open countryside as a result of modern farming methods, and it is important to try and compensate for that wherever possible. It's probably true to say that if it weren't for gardens, frogs and toads would be extinct by now in large parts of the country. Encouraging them is therefore a worthwhile conservation exercise that makes a real difference. The second point relates to what frogs and toads eat (see p. 150). Basically, this includes most things that gardeners are keen to get rid of: slugs and snails particularly, but also a whole host of plant-eating insects. The more frogs and toads in a garden, the more flowers, lettuces, etc., you are likely to keep each year – simple economics.

Q: What should I do to make my garden popular with frogs?

A: That's simple: build a pond. The presence of a breeding site will attract adults in spring, and these and their offspring are likely to spend a large part of their time in your garden from then onwards. There are some other things you can do too, though none is as important as the pond (which is, of course, an attractive garden feature anyway). Rockeries, with creeping plants, provide cover in the summer and will encourage frogs to stay in your garden rather than a neighbour's. If your garden wall is a Colditz type, with no holes or gaps around the bottom, then frogs obviously won't be able to get in or out. You might be able to maintain a small population entirely within your garden, but it isn't very satisfactory and a good plan is to make a few small holes in your wall or fence at ground level. Mowing the lawn is another thing it pays to be a bit careful about. When tiny frogs leave the pond each summer they can easily get minced by lawnmowers, and the best way to avoid this is just by being a good gardener: if you mow regularly the grass is kept too short for the froglets' liking, and they won't stay in it. Mowing only occasionally is more dangerous because longer grass probably will have froglets hiding away somewhere.

Q: How do I make a pond suitable for frogs and toads?

A: Almost any garden pond is likely to be OK for frogs – they don't seem very fussy, but there are certainly things you can do to make a *good* frog pond rather than one which is just 'alright'. The basics of pond construction are explained in most gardening books; there are several materials available these days, including fibreglass, plastic and concrete, of which I find the flexible plastic or rubber sheeting types to be the most convenient. Butyl is undoubtedly the best of these, but also the most expensive. It is very resistant to accidental damage, though, and once in place should last a lifetime (whereas you have to replace the plastic sheeting). A few points to think about when designing the pond are:

Size: Basically the bigger the better, but even quite small ponds will be used by frogs. I have seen baby baths sunk in gardens which regularly attract 1 or 2 pairs of frogs each year, but something like 3 × 4 yards (3 × 4 metres) is a good size and probably the minimum needed for a chance of attracting toads.

Shape: Lots of scope for individual taste, but try and include a very shallow area (3–4 inches, 7.5–10 cm) because frogs like to spawn in such places. Maximum depth should be enough to prevent the pond freezing solid in a severe winter – say 24 inches (60 cm) – because that would kill any frogs hibernating there.

Position: Put the pond in as sunny a spot as possible. It will look nicer, tadpoles do better in warm water, and you won't have trouble fishing out dead leaves every autumn if there are no trees too close.

Surroundings: It's a good idea to leave a bit of long grass, or some ornamental rockery plants, around the pond edge; don't make it too tidy. Cover from plants helps baby frogs and toads to get out of the water without being eaten by blackbirds and other predators.

Waterweed: Plant up with the usual types of oxygenators (submerged plants, like Canadian pondweed) and a few marginals, like irises. Frogs really aren't fussy, so do what pleases you.

Other pond dwellers: Many pond creatures are becoming rare apart from frogs and toads, and it's a good idea to encourage dragonflies, water snails, beetles, newts and other beasties. Some of these eat tadpoles, but only on a small scale – they won't seriously endanger your frog population. Fish, unfortunately, are another matter. Goldfish and other types commonly put in garden ponds wreak havoc with tadpoles, and if you're keen on frogs it is really much better to have no fish at all. A pond without fish is actually much more interesting, because so many other kinds of creatures can then live in it. If you do keep fish you may still get some frogs, but they will be much less successful as a result. Toads, on the other hand, don't do so badly (because of their nasty-tasting tadpoles) and can do quite well in large fish ponds. Newts suffer worst of all, and it's rare to see more than the odd one or two in a pond containing fish. One possible solution to the problem of mixing fish and amphibians in the same pond is to segregate part of the pool with plastic netting

that fish can't get through. This can work quite well if done properly, but goldfish are particularly clever at finding gaps when there is the incentive of a tadpole dinner on the other side.

Q: Do I need to do anything else?

A: It's a good plan to introduce deliberately a few clumps of frog spawn, or strings of toad spawn, rather than just wait for them to 'arrive'. If possible these should be obtained from a friend's existing garden pond; if you do have to take from the wild, only remove a little of what is available so as not to endanger the colony. Most people find that frog spawn is easier to come by than toad spawn, and that frogs establish themselves better in gardens. But it's always worth trying with toads too, especially if you have a large pond. Another way of starting your colony is by putting an 'advert' for spawn in your local newsagent's window round about March time – you may be surprised at how much you get offered. Simply place the spawn in your pond, and leave it to do its thing; no more attention than that should be necessary, and within a couple of years your first 'offspring' should be coming back to breed of their own accord.

Keeping frogs and toads

Most schoolchildren keep frog spawn and tadpoles at some time in their lives. The point here is: how much should this sort of thing be encouraged? Natterjacks are of course protected by law, so keeping them is out of the question, but common frogs and toads and their spawn are often there for the taking. Some people hold the view that wild animals should always be left alone, and certainly nothing should be done that might endanger a population. And, of course, it's important not to be cruel to any individuals. With these provisos, I think there is much to be said for keeping a few tadpoles and watching them turn into frogs or toads. It's a great learning experience, and if done properly will actually benefit rather than harm the species in question. The key phrase, of course, is 'done properly'. It is difficult to rear baby frogs after the metamorphosis stage and I wouldn't recommend trying it without the help of someone experienced, but keeping one or two adults is fairly straightforward. If you really want to have a go at this, there are a few more questions that need to be answered.

Q: Where should I get my spawn or tadpoles?

A: Preferably, a friend's garden pond. If you don't know of any such source, only take from a 'wild' pond if there is so much spawn there that removing a bit won't make any significant difference. In any case, it's important not to take too much because overcrowding will slow down tadpole growth and can kill them all off under extreme conditions. All you need is about half a teacupful of spawn, or maybe 100 tadpoles; more than that will just end up being wasted. Carry them home carefully, in a small bucket of water or something similar.

Q: How should I keep them?

A: This amount of spawn or tadpoles can be put in a small aquarium tank with clean tap water (which has first been allowed to stand a day or so, to remove chlorine). The tank should be in a fairly sunny position, perhaps even outside in the garden (but cover it with netting to stop birds getting a free dinner); adding a few water plants isn't a bad idea. Tadpoles need food; the best things to give are bits of *boiled* lettuce leaves, or the pellets sold in petshops for rabbits. I have always found these pellets to be particularly cheap and convenient. The key thing is not to pollute the water by adding too much food; for 100 tadpoles, about 5 good-sized pellets every 3–4 days should be enough. Change the water every week or two, sooner if it starts to get murky. As the taddies grow, make sure there is something the baby frogs or toads can climb out onto when they metamorphose. They drown very easily at this stage, and are generally fragile. When the front legs start to appear, a good plan is to tip the tank up a bit making the water at one end very shallow, and then put a bank of damp earth there sticking out of the water. The new froglets or toadlets should be released as soon as possible in some place providing suitable cover, such as long, damp grass in a corner of the garden. Try to avoid carrying them far at this stage, but if you must transport them, use damp grass or moss in a box. Never put them back in water, or they will speedily drown, and never let them get too warm by putting them in direct sunlight.

Q: What about adult frogs and toads?

A: Frogs and toads should not be disturbed at their breeding sites, and pairs especially should be left alone. However, the odd animal found later in summer can be kept quite satisfactorily in a suitable enclosure – these are known as 'vivaria' in the trade. A vivarium can be anything from an old wooden box with lid added, to one of the more elaborate metal types sold in petshops. The important features are that it should allow air in through some sort of grille or mesh, and be escape-proof (it's worth remembering not just that frogs can jump, but also that toads can climb). Moist earth with one or two sheltered places (flat stones or bits of wood, with gaps underneath), a few plants and a dish of water that the animals can easily climb in and out of are the essential furnishings. The whole thing should be of a decent size – at least 2 square feet (60 square cm) of ground surface for 2 or 3 frogs or toads – and sited in a cool, shady place out of direct sunshine. Better than these, though, are the much larger 'outdoor vivaria' which are quite big bits of garden suitably laid out with pond, plants, hidey-holes, etc., and surrounded by an escape-proof fence. But these are for the real enthusiast, and not necessary just for a bit of short-term observation. Frogs and toads in vivaria must of course be supplied with food, such as worms or beetles, every few days and any individuals showing no interest in food within a few days of capture should be released promptly. In any case, I wouldn't recommend keeping frogs or toads in small vivaria for more than a month or two; they should really be wild and free. Indeed, wherever possible it's very much better to make a garden pond (see p. 98) and just encourage wild populations to become established. You'll see more of the life cycle, won't have to provide any food, and reap the benefits in the control of garden pests as well as carrying out a useful piece of conservation.

Illegal immigrants

Up to now we have mainly considered just the three native species of frogs and toads – those we believe have a long history in Britain, going back at least to the end of the last Ice Age. There are, however, a few newcomers on the scene. Either accidentally or on purpose, man has liberated alien species into the British countryside on many occasions over the last 150 years and a few have survived to establish themselves. Best known, and the one with the longest pedigree, is the European edible frog, *Rana esculenta*. Enormous numbers of this species were

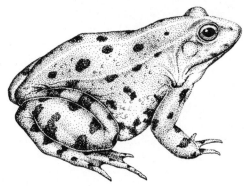

Edible frog

brought over from France and Belgium during the last century, apparently in wicker baskets, and released in the Fens and other parts of East Anglia. Colonies became established in several places but they never spread very far, and usually they eventually died out. However, a thriving population was discovered recently in Norfolk (actually of the closely-related species, *Rana lessonae*), very close to one of the first release sites, so the animals here may be descendants of this original stock. Earlier in the present century more colonies got going in south-east England, and I know of one in Surrey doing very well indeed: thousands of edible frogs live in an old clay pit, and in late spring their croaking is little short of deafening. These are very aquatic frogs and seldom move far from the water's edge, where they like to bask in the sun and jump in with a loud plop when disturbed.

Edible frogs are a little larger than our common frogs, and often have bright green backs and sides. Bigger still is a more recent introduction, the marsh frog, *Rana ridibunda*. Indeed, this is the largest of all the European frogs (adults can be up to 5 inches, 125 mm, long and weigh up to 11 oz, 300 g), with a darker green body but otherwise rather similar habits to *R. esculenta*. It's also Britain's most successful amphibian introduction: just 12 adults were brought from Hungary and

Marsh frog

released on the edge of Romney Marsh in 1935, since when their descendants have spread all over Romney as well as other low-lying areas of Kent and Sussex. They like to live along the edges of the ditches which are so numerous in these flat, marshy districts, and still seem to be expanding their range. Within the last ten years they have appeared only a few miles from my home, adding a little more interest to the local amphibian scene. So noisy are they that local residents even raised the question in the House of Commons of whether they could be silenced, thus far without any consequence for the frogs concerned. People have also been worried that they might harm our native species, but although they are certainly big enough to eat newts and small common frogs, recent studies have shown that marsh frogs only live in habitats which our natives don't much like. So they rarely meet, and there doesn't seem to be a lot of harm done in this particular regard. Of course we don't know what effects large numbers of these big frogs might be having on other interesting beasts, like dragonflies for example, and it would seem a good idea for someone to try and find out.

Only three other species have shown any ability to survive and breed in Britain for more than a few years. One well established immigrant is the remarkable midwife toad, *Alytes obstetricans*, introduced accidentally to a garden in Bedford-

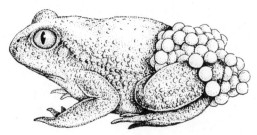

Male midwife toad, carrying eggs.

shire with a consignment of water plants nearly 100 years ago. They're still there, but haven't spread. Midwife toads are smaller than our common toads and equally drab-looking in colour. Their interesting feature is the way they breed: rather than just laying spawn in ponds, the males carry the eggs around with them, twisted around their hindlegs and on their backs, until they are ready to hatch. European tree frogs, *Hyla arborea*, are small, bright green, and quite incredibly noisy. Their

European tree frog

calls are like a cross between a dog barking and a duck quacking, and I hate to think how unpopular frogs would become if they were ever widespread in England. But this doesn't seem very likely; despite many attempts to introduce them, the only colony known to have existed for a long time is a tiny population living around a single pond in the New Forest. This has become a bit of a mecca for herpetologists – conveniently situated next to a pub – and it remains to be seen how well the tree frogs survive all the attention they are now getting. Finally, and perhaps the most alien of all, is the South African clawed toad, *Xenopus laevis*. This entirely aquatic

Xenopus

and (at least to my mind) singularly unattractive-looking amphibian has survived and bred in a few ponds on the Isle of Wight for nearly twenty years, and recently a much larger colony was discovered in a Welsh valley. No one knows how long they have been there, but *Xenopus* is widely used in research and large numbers have been imported into Britain for decades past. They are secretive beasts, and there may well be other wild populations that no one has noticed yet.

Whether these recent additions to our frog and toad fauna are a good or a bad thing is open to debate. Everyone has their own opinion; it's a bit like asking your doctor whether vitamin C tablets are good for you. What is certain, though, is that since the Wildlife and Countryside Act of 1981 deliberate introduction of these or any other animals into Britain is against the law. The powers-that-be have decided to err on the safe side, though whether a parliamentary statute will have any actual effect on how animals distribute themselves in future (with or without a bit of help from man) remains to be seen.

Marine toads: the amphibian rabbit

When you think of the species that have been introduced to new countries by man, and subsequently become pests, the ones which spring most readily to mind are usually mammals. Grey squirrels, black and brown rats, coypu and mink are all well known examples in Britain, and you could add rabbits in Australia, goats in the Galapagos islands, and many more. How many people would consider putting an amphibian at the top of this list of human follies? Yet, in terms of extent of spread, this is the rightful place of the marine toad, Bufo marinus, *which looks like a giant version of our common toad and was originally native only to parts of Central and South America. It doesn't, by the way, live in the sea – another case of silly*

naming in the amphibian world.

In this century, however, its spread by the hand of man – as a 'controller' of insect pests – has been unequalled by most, if not all, the mammals listed earlier. Few parts of the tropics are now without

this lugubrious creature, which seems to thrive almost wherever it is released. Africa, Asia, Indonesia and Australia all now have their marine toads, and usually expanding populations of them. In Australia, for example, they were first released in Queensland but within the last few years have spread as far as Darwin on the north coast. Unfortunately they're not much good at what the farmers intended them for – pest control in growing crops – but do seem horribly efficient at killing off native species of amphibians, some of which may be getting rare as a result. Certainly my impression of Queensland was that you can find ten marine toads for every other sort of amphibian put together, at least in the coastal belt. Like so many introduced species that take off and do well, control has proved an impossible task. However, at least some imaginative uses have been made of them; market places in northern Australia now usually have a stall with models and ornaments made – you've guessed it – from leathery marine toad skin. Bufo marinus has found for itself a small and rather gruesome role in the outback economy.

Frogs in the kitchen

Mention the eating of frogs' legs, and most of us would make an immediate connection with France and the habits of Frenchmen. Unfortunately for the frogs, this is not by any means the limit of their culinary appeal and they are consumed by many peoples all over the world. It is difficult to imagine a less tasty-looking morsel than African clawed toads, yet these are widely eaten (although in many places considered suitable only for the womenfolk). Frogs are deemed a luxury in China, and a wide variety of frog and toad species are collected for the pot in South America. For the Australian bushmen frogs are even more versatile; not only are they eaten, but some species dig themselves into the sand with a reservoir of water inside them. The aborigines have learnt how to find this living drink, and readily use the hapless frogs when no other source of water is available.

In Europe the habit of eating frogs' legs goes back a long time. The Romans probably did it (according to Sir Christopher Lever this may have resulted in their very early introduction to Britain); while monks have also been blamed for introducing the edible frog into Britain in the Middle Ages as a source of pastoral protein. More recently it is true that frogs' legs have become a part of *haute cuisine* mainly in France and Belgium, but even as long ago as the turn of the century

fricassée de grenouilles were on sale in the West End of London. The European edible frog no doubt attained its culinary popularity on account of it being so conspicuous as well as abundant over much of the Continent; it is so common that the banks of many ponds in France look like miniature Mediterranean beaches, packed with frogs soaking up the sun on a warm summer's day. For ages the traditional way of catching frogs for the pot was with a fishing rod and line, baited simply with a bit of coloured cloth waved about over the water. Edible frogs leap at anything that moves, and a skilful fisherman can flick them out and straight into his waiting free hand; no hook is needed. It's just as well they are so common, because a decent meal for one person requires the legs from 15–20 animals. Nor was it just edible frogs that were eaten, either. Our own common frogs also used to suffer the same fate, because they came out of hibernation earlier than the edible ones do and were immediately pounced on by gourmets suffering from a long winter abstinence. Apparently the flavours of the two species cannot be told apart. Ironically, most European countries now protect their amphibians from this kind of thing and the market for frogs' legs is increasingly catered for by Asian species. The extent of this trade, especially in the Indian bullfrog, *Rana tigrina*, is quite astonishing, and anyone ordering frogs' legs in a restaurant today is more likely to find the limbs of this animal than any other on their plate. Exports from India to Britain alone amounted to 32 tonnes in 1980, the equivalent of more than 100,000 animals, and all this to one of the minor importers. More than half of India's exports go to EEC countries, while consumption is rising in the USA, Canada and Japan.

There are obviously important moral questions in all this. The whole process can be barbarically cruel, live animals simply being chopped in half to obtain the edible portions while throwing away the rest. So it's bad for the individual frogs concerned, but what about the populations? Is such an enormous rate of collection threatening frogs with extinction? The European edible frog has evidently survived centuries of persecution, but never on the scale now being visited upon some of the Asian species. Although the evidence isn't very clear yet, it looks as if some areas of

India are being depleted of frogs by local people who find their collection and sale a valuable source of income. One result has been an increase in insect pests for the paddy farmers, and an increased reliance on expensive artificial pesticides supplied by multinational, western-based companies. It all sounds like another case of Third World exploitation, and efforts are being made to restrict the trade. Of course frog farming could be developed, but there are dangers in stimulating a luxury appetite which may grow faster than farm production and continue to wreak havoc among wild populations. Those who have tasted frogs' legs generally speak of a similarity to chicken, so the flavour scarcely seems to justify the appalling rate of attrition currently permitted. Let's hope the world will one day be able to do without frog meat.

All for a few nights' sleep

Not many people know that frogs played a part in the French Revolution. This wasn't, as you might imagine, because supplies of frogs' legs were hogged by the aristocracy, but more on account of their noisy habits. The story goes that peasants were made to stay up and 'beat the water' all night in the breeding season to keep the frogs quiet, thereby allowing their masters a comfortable night's sleep. Difficult to imagine a situation more conducive to the plotting of a revolution.

Folklore

Frogs and toads don't feature a lot in folklore, and when they do it is usually in an uncomplimentary context. Not to put too fine a point on it, they've been pretty much despised by all and sundry. The Old Testament probably holds the record for the most ancient mention of frogs – they were one of Moses's plagues. They got into the houses of the Egyptians, into their bed chambers and their kneading (bread) troughs – a miserable nuisance for fastidious people, especially when the frogs died all over the place. Curiously, though toads might seem more offensive, there is no mention of them in the Bible. If the tale has any truth it probably relates either to a breeding migration of adults (see p. 67) or to a mass dispersal of froglets from pond banks after metamorphosis (see p. 83). A wise pharaoh would of course have been grateful for this and not at all cross, since a good frog year should spell fewer insect pests and a better harvest. Perhaps he was, as this particular act evidently did not have the desired effect.

An associated story is that of 'raining frogs', tales of which still get around from time to time, especially in the tropics. Probably this too stems from masses of frogs or froglets becoming active during a normal rainstorm, appearing all over the place as if from nowhere, to revel in the warm and humid conditions. It has been suggested that freak whirlwinds could pick up large numbers of frogs and then drop them somewhere else, but I've yet to hear a convincing account to back up this idea.

Topsel (1858) reviews the culinary and medicinal properties of frogs and says it was believed that if you wanted to know the secrets from a woman, you should cut out the tongue from a live frog and put it on the woman's heart; then ask her your question, and she will confess all. But Topsel (evidently willing to accept many such ideas) comments that if this one were true ('magical foolery' he calls it) we 'had more need of frogs than of Justices of the Peace and Magistrates'. He also recounts that some do write that if a woman takes a frog into her mouth she will not conceive that year. I think we should not take too much notice of that either. Oil and salt and frogs make a potion, he says, good for gout and also a cure for poisons.

There was an old yarn that toads contained a jewel in their heads – something akin to pearls in oysters, I suppose. I hate to think how many toads may have been murdered to disprove this notion, which must surely stem from the beautifully-marked orange-gold irises in their eyes.

But the general view of these creatures is relayed in the *Macbeth* witch's cauldron, with 'toad, that under the cold stone, days and nights has thirty-one, swelter'd venom sleeping got, boil thou first i' the charmed pot'. Newts and frogs were added later. It wasn't just laymen that had it in for them, either. Linnaeus, the great classifier of biology, took the trouble to point out how much he disliked amphibians and reptiles and Thomas Penant (author of Britain's first proper book of zoology in 1776) described toads as 'the most deformed and hideous of all animals – objects of detestation'. To a thoroughly objective herpetologist it's impossible to understand how all these people could be so misguided, but public relations is still something of a problem for frogs and toads. They can't change their image; it's up to us to look upon them in a more enlightened way.

One of the older uses of frogs and toads — ingredients in a witch's brew.

Research on frogs and toads

After so long in the wilderness, research into frog and toad biology 'in the field' is attracting much more attention now. I think there are a number of reasons for this; firstly, because they have been so neglected in the past there is still quite a lot to learn about them – straightforward study projects. Secondly, they're relatively easy animals to study (at least, they are at some times of year), without expensive or elaborate equipment. And, thirdly, it is being realized that in many areas they play important roles in community ecology.

All sorts of things are now being done. At the 'simple' end of the scale, people are surveying ponds and ditches to find out which species breeds where, and (we hope) why. Nobody really understands what makes toads spawn in one pond, frogs in another, and none at all in some pools. This entails finding answers to questions such as: how important are various fish species, as potential tadpole predators, to the distribution of amphibians? What is the significance of the terrestrial habitat around a breeding pond? And many, many more. Another popular approach is the complete fencing off of a particular pond, together with pitfall traps, followed by the very careful study of the frogs, toads and newts going in and out during the breeding season. This can tell us things like: how many frogs going into a pond never come out again (i.e. die or are killed there)? How many of the eggs that are laid survive to become froglets or toadlets? And so on. More advanced studies may involve looking at sections of toe bones under the microscope to find out the ages of individuals, and ultimately the age structure of a population; do frogs in different places have different life expectancies? And there is the business of radio-tracking, fitting animals with small transmitters and then following them around: how far do toads go each night, and where? Where do they hibernate? Behaviour, too, is a fascinating area of research. It's intriguing to find out why some male frogs and toads mate with several females each spring, while others get none. Is this because some males are better fighters, or do females make a choice on their own criteria?

Apart from general interest, some of this research has applications – particularly to conservation. For example, in the case of the rare natterjack it has become very important to know just what is needed to keep a population healthy, in terms of design of breeding ponds, management of trees and scrub, and things like that. Research being carried out now could have a major impact on the future of frogs and toads in Britain. It's never easy to get money – frog research isn't high on the list of most grant-awarding authorities' priorities – but some has been provided recently, especially by the Nature Conservancy Council, World Wildlife Fund,

Natural Environment Research Council and the Vincent Wildlife Trust. Nevertheless, funding is likely to be a limiting factor for the foreseeable future.

It's worth stressing how much fun research is. Frogs and toads are such good subjects that almost anyone with a mind to do a bit of background reading, and a little thinking of course, can carry out work likely to tell us something previously unknown about these animals. And there's a lot of satisfaction in that.

For example, just recording a species in a new place is a valuable thing to do and in Britain an institution known as the Biological Records Centre at Abbots Ripton, Huntingdonshire, welcomes all such information. Garden ponds are great places for a bit of homework on amphibians living under virtually wild conditions; you can count how the numbers of frogspawn clumps vary from year to year, how many eggs fail to develop properly, and loads of other things. Imagination is the main limiting factor here.

Frogs, toads and medicine

Just occasionally even frog research throws up something of applied value to everyday life. This happened most spectacularly some forty years ago, when it was discovered that African clawed toads (Xenopus) could be used as accurate predictors of early human pregnancy. Injection of a small volume of urine from a woman in

the first few months of pregnancy into a female Xenopus *causes the toad to lay eggs within twenty-four hours; the response is to small amounts of a hormone present in the urine, and for many years this became a standard medical test. Of course it was a bit cumbersome having to keep tankfuls of toads around the place and the technique has now been replaced by even quicker chemical methods. Nevertheless, a lot of people alive today were first revealed to the world as a bunch of toad eggs in a laboratory tank.*

Work being done on

Gastrodema, *which broods tadpoles in its stomach (see p. 15),* *(see p. 15)* *is intended to discover how acid secretions from the stomach wall are suppressed for the duration, because herein may lie a potential preventive for human duodenal ulcers caused by excess acid secretions of the stomach on the wall of the duodenum.*

The Times *reported in 1984 that 'The Chinese government once ran a campaign to get women to swallow live tadpoles as a means of birth control. The tadpoles proved unreliable, however, and the government desisted.'*

National societies

Anyone seriously interested in frogs or toads – or newts or reptiles for that matter – is well advised to join a herpetological society. There are several such societies in Britain, of which (being a member) I would recommend the British Herpetological Society as the most active and with the broadest range of interests. Everything from captive breeding through to active field research and conservation is catered for, with regular meetings and publications sent out free to members keeping them up-to-date with news and developments. It's a place to share an interest; it's also a way of becoming involved in conservation, for which tasks volunteers are welcomed most readily. Details can be obtained from the Secretary, British Herpetological Society, Zoological Society of London, Regents Park, London NW1 4RY.

Bibliography

Books on amphibians tend to be rather few and far between. Some of the more recent ones are listed below, but not all are still in print. For these you will have to resort to a library or a good second-hand bookshop.

1. *The British Amphibians and Reptiles*, by Malcolm Smith, in the New Naturalist series published by Collins. Several editions between 1951 and 1973. Excellent reading, and highly recommended.

2. *Reptiles and Amphibians in Britain*, by Deryk Frazer. A New Naturalist update of Smith's book, published in 1983. Contains some additional information but omits parts of the basic biology given by Smith.

3. *The Ecology and Life History of the Common Frog*, by Maxwell Savage. Published by Pitmans (London) in 1961. A thorough and fascinating account of the life and times of *Rana temporaria*.

4. *The Natterjack Toad*, by Trevor Beebee. Published by Oxford University Press in 1983. A monograph of the general biology and natural history of *Bufo calamita*.

5. *A Field Guide to the Reptiles and Amphibians of Britain and Europe*, by E. Arnold, J. Burton and D. Ovenden. Published by Collins in 1978. An invaluable aid to identification of all the life-stages, particularly for anyone holidaying in Europe where there are so many more species to cope with.

Index